Cinders & Smoke

A
Mile by Mile Guide®
for the
Durango and Silverton Narrow Gauge Railroad

by
Doris B. Osterwald

P9-AOU-838

Western Guideways, Ltd.

Publisher – Guidebooks · Railroad and Western History
PO Box 343 · Hugo, Colorado 80821 · 719/743-6818

CINDERS & SMOKE

A Mile by Mile Guide®
for the
Durango and Silverton Narrow Gauge Railroad

Eighth Edition, Copyright© 2001 by Western Guideways, Ltd.
Thirty-fifth printing, 2004

All rights reserved.
No part of this book may be reproduced or transmitted in any form or by any means, electronic or mechanical, including photocopying, recording, or by any information retrieval system, now or in the future, without permission in writing from the publisher.

ISBN: 0-931788-80-3

Electronic Imagesetting and Printing by:
Golden Bell Press
Denver, Colorado

Printed in the United States of America

TABLE OF CONTENTS

Acknowledgments

Without the support and encouragement of officials of the former Denver & Rio Grande Western Railroad and the management of the two succeeding owners of the Durango & Silverton Narrow Gauge Railroad, this book would never have grown and survived from its first modest printing of 94 pages in 1965. I have enjoyed each and every year of watching and riding **The Silverton** as it winds its way along the Animas River between Durango and Silverton. It is most rewarding to have written a book that remains popular after all these years. My thanks to each and every reader.

My heartfelt thanks to each of my family for putting up with my fascination with narrow gauge railroading and in helping prepare this Eighth Edition. Sons Carl and Ray carefully revised the section on locomotives and operating procedures. (This facet of railroading is beyond my ken!) Carl also worked his magic editing and laying out the text on the computer. Grandson, Ren Osterwald, took the new cover photograph of No. 486 during RAILFEST 2000. Daughter Becky and daughter-in-law April, carefully proofed the entire book.

D&SNG Conductor Richard Millard, Museum Coordinator, Jeff Ellingson, Vice President of Marketing, Kristi Nelson Cohen and her Assistant, Mary Jo Rakowski were always ready to answer my questions and offered many suggestions. Charles Albi and Kenton Forrest of the Colorado Railroad Museum and Del McCoy of Sundance Publications contributed their expertise on new facets of railroading included in this edition. Frank Adler, owner of the Sallie Bowman mine, shared data on that old prospect. My heartfelt thanks to Jeff Johnson, former D&SNG engineer who now works for the Union Pacific Railroad, for his careful and thorough editing of the entire manuscript. Thanks also to each of the photographers who graciously permitted me to include their work.

In addition to the thrill of listening to a steam engine laboring up a steep grade, the melodious sound of a whistle echoing across the Animas Canyon, or the dubious delight of having cinders and smoke land on my face, the people met and the friends made are very special. The list grows with each passing year.

—DBO, May 2001

INTRODUCTION

Welcome aboard the Durango & Silverton Narrow Gauge Railroad. You are about to embark on an unforgettable narrow gauge steam rail journey along the spectacular and ever-changing Animas River. This somewhat nostalgic means of transportation is a relic of earlier times. If the first few flakes of placer gold had not been discovered at Silverton in 1860, and if the Denver & Rio Grande Railway had not decided to expand its narrow gauge system to the growing mining camp along the Animas River, your trip would not be possible today.

The Silverton generally follows the Animas River as it meanders back and forth across the lovely lower valley. But beyond Baker's Bridge this slow-moving character changes to that of a river running wild through an almost inaccessible gorge. Past the gorge, the track continues to follow the rushing, tumbling Animas to Silverton. The distinctive greenish color of the water probably is due to copper salts from mines in the Silverton area.

Beyond Rockwood, the only access to the canyon is by train, foot, horseback, kayak, or raft. The remote and incredibly beautiful, glacially-carved peaks and cirque basins of the Weminuche Wilderness are visible from the train—if you look up. These 13,000 to 14,000 ft (3,900 to 4,200 m) mountain peaks are some of the most rugged and inaccessible of any in Colorado. As your train labors up grade, you may not be aware that these awesome, towering peaks stand at least one mile above the bottom of the canyon. Each mile of your journey brings forth vistas of the majestic snow-capped peaks, small, secluded mountain parks, vertical avalanche tracks, and the remains of former mines, all of which make for a memorable experience.

When gold was discovered in Colorado in 1859, only fine particles and flakes were recovered with placer mining. After more complex ores were located in lode deposits, it was necessary to separate the gold from worthless rock, using arrastras and stamp mills (see p. 88), before it could be shipped to eastern smelters. Pack trains could carry only the richest ores across the mountains on narrow, indistinct trails that had been used by animals and Indians for centuries. As new strikes were made, mining camps sprang up almost overnight. Trails gradually were improved and became narrow, rutted roads. Freight wagons, pulled by oxen or mules, made slow, laborious trips back and forth carrying ore, mining machinery, and other essentials to the growing communities.

By June 1870, when the Denver Pacific Railroad steamed into Denver from Cheyenne, Wyoming, mining camps all over Colorado starting dreaming of rail service to link their infant towns with Denver. The Denver Pacific connected with the recently completed transcontinental Union Pacific Railroad in Cheyenne. Railroads could carry passengers, heavy mining machinery, equipment, coal, lumber, ores, and other freight more efficiently than pack trains or wagons. Profits from such operations were expected to pay for construction and leave handsome dividends for stockholders.

The Denver & Rio Grande Railway Company (D&RG) was incorporated in the Territories of Colorado and New Mexico October 27, 1870, to build a railroad from Denver south to El Paso, Texas. The company also planned to extend rails to Mexico City, Mexico. The route to El Paso was to go south to Pueblo, west through the Arkansas River Canyon (Royal Gorge), across Poncha Pass and into the San Luis Valley to the Rio Grande River. Tracks were to follow the Rio Grande southward to El Paso. Six branches were planned to the mining areas of Colorado, and one branch was projected to reach Salt Lake City, Utah. The San Juan Extension was to be built to Silverton, a booming mining town in the San Juans. The route selected meandered back and forth along the Colorado-New Mexico border, past easily available coal and timber supplies, in which the Rio Grande invested and developed. President of this first narrow gauge railroad in Colorado was General William Jackson Palmer, who served in the Civil War with distinction and came west after the war to work on the Kansas Pacific Railroad. This line reached Denver August 15, 1870.

The Rio Grande decided to build its railroad "narrow gauge" (rails 3 feet apart) rather than "standard gauge" (rails 4 feet, 8½ inches apart) which was the standard on most other U.S. railroads. The choice was made because narrow gauge construction was cheaper—equipment cost less and sharper curves were possible and thus it was better suited to mountainous terrain. The railroad was only 11 years old when Palmer and his associates realized they were bucking great odds with a narrow gauge main line operation. Consequently, by 1890, the major narrow gauge westward route via Leadville and Tennessee Pass had been converted to standard gauge. Portions of the original main line to Salt Lake City across Marshall Pass and through Gunnison, Colorado, remained narrow gauge until abandonment in 1955. Standard gauge rail was laid to Antonito in 1901, thus dual gauging a portion of the original San Juan Extension. The D&RG experienced years of financial turmoil and bankruptcy proceedings, and in 1921 it was reorganized as Denver & Rio Grande Western Railroad (D&RGW).

The San Juan Extension managed to survive until the late 1960s, but **The Silverton** was the only portion of the route that showed a profit, as tourists and railfans discovered the pleasure of a leisurely rail journey along the Animas River to Silverton. In 1968, the Interstate Commerce Commission approved the abandonment of the narrow gauge between Antonito and Durango. The last revenue train left Alamosa westbound for Durango in Dec. 1968, with No. 473 pulling several coaches and dead K-36 No. 481. Through the efforts of many individuals, preservation societies and towns, the Colorado-New Mexico Railroad Authorities were organized, and by July 1970, the two states purchased the line between Antonito, Colorado, and Chama, New Mexico. This section of the narrow gauge operates as the Cumbres & Toltec Scenic Railroad (C&TS). The other portions of the San Juan Extension were abandoned in 1970.

On June 1, 1967, the National Park Service designated the Silverton Branch of the D&RGW Railroad as a National Historical Landmark. In March 1968, the Silverton Branch also was designated as a National Historic Civil Engineering Landmark by the American Society of Civil Engineers. This award recognizes the tremendous part played by the civil engineering profession in surveying and constructing the branch through the difficult winter and spring of 1881-82. Then, on July 11, 1982, the National Railway Historical Society dedicated a beautiful granite monument at Cascade Canyon Wye. This dedication was made exactly 100 years after passenger service commenced on the Silverton Branch of the San Juan Extension (p. 94).

The D&RGW continued to operate the Silverton Branch as an isolated segment of its once vast narrow gauge system until 1981, when the line was purchased by Charles E. Bradshaw, Jr. and renamed the Durango & Silverton Narrow Gauge Railroad. The D&SNG expanded passenger service from the former two trains per day operated by the D&RGW to at least four daily excursion trains during the busy summer months.

In March 1997 the D&SNG was sold to First American Railways, Inc., headquartered in Hollywood, Florida. The railroad was sold again in 1998 to American Heritage Railways (p. 103-104).

When the Silverton Branch opened for business in July 1882, those first travelers probably never would have thought it possible that 100 years later more than 200,000 people would travel along the same route each year. One wonders if those early passengers were as awestruck by the incredible beauty of this remote canyon surrounded by the magnificent peaks of the Needle Mountains and the Grenadier Range as are today's visitors.

USING THE MILE BY MILE GUIDE®

The Mile by Mile Guide® describes scenic highlights and points of interest along the railroad and is keyed to mileposts and U.S. Forest Service signs near the track. Nine guide maps are included that illustrate the railroad route in sections. The Index Map on page 9 shows the Durango-Silverton region and the positions of the overlapping guide maps.

The mileposts are numbered signs, visible from two directions, on slender steel posts (see photo on back cover) that are spaced one mile apart along the right side of the train going toward Silverton, and the left side of the train going towards Durango. Numbers on the mileposts indicate the distance by rail from Denver, where the D&RG started in 1870. Thus, at the time the railroad was built, there were 451.5 miles of track from Denver to the Durango depot, and 496.7 miles to the Silverton depot.

To aid in locating the points of interest on the guide maps, the railroad route is drawn with cross-ties 1/10 mile apart. Entries in the guide text show the mileage at each point to the nearest 1/20 of a mile.

GEOLOGIC SYMBOLS:

Patterns in a light-tan color are used indicate different geologic formations on the guide maps. Names of the formations use the standard geologic abbreviations listed below. The uppercase letter indicates the age of the formation, while the lower-case lettering is geologic shorthand for the name of the formation or rock unit. The formations are explained in greater detail in the Columnar Section, pp. 84-85.

Quaternary Period:

Qal	Alluvium, gravel, boulders, soils along streams
Qg	Terrace gravels
Qls	Landslides; loose rocks and soil that have moved downhill
Qm	Moraines; loose rock debris left by retreating glaciers

Tertiary Period:

Ti	Quartz monzonite porphyry and other intrusive volcanic rocks
Tv	Extrusive volcanic rocks

Cretaceous Period:

Kmv	Mesaverde Group of sedimentary rocks
Km	Mancos Shale
Kd	Dakota Sandstone

Jurassic Period:

J	A number of sedimentary formations grouped together

Upper Triassic and Permian Periods:

R	Redbeds of the Dolores, Cutler, and Rico Formations

Pennsylvanian Period:

Ph	Hermosa Group
Pm	Molas Formation

Upper Devonian Period:

D	Ouray and Elbert Formations

Upper Cambrian Period:

€i	Ignacio Quartzite

Precambrian Period:

p€g	Granite
p€u	Uncompahgre Formation
p€gb	Gabbro
p€sg	Ancient schists, gneisses

8

INDEX MAP

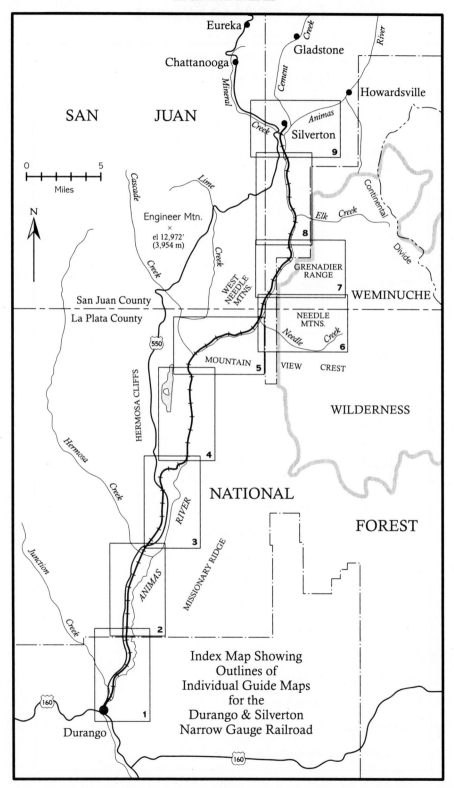

Eureka

Chattanooga

Gladstone

Howardsville

SAN   JUAN

Mineral

Creek

Cement Creek

Animas River

Silverton

9

Cascade

Lime

Creek

Engineer Mtn.
×
el 12,972'
(3,954 m)

Creek

Creek

Elk Creek

8

Continental

Divide

WEST
NEEDLE
MTNS.

GRENADIER
RANGE

7

WEMINUCHE

San Juan County

La Plata County

NEEDLE
MTNS.

Needle Creek

6

550

MOUNTAIN

5

VIEW

CREST

WILDERNESS

Hermosa

Creek

HERMOSA CLIFFS

4

RIVER

NATIONAL

FOREST

Junction

ANIMAS

MISSIONARY RIDGE

3

Creek

2

160

1

Index Map Showing
Outlines of
Individual Guide Maps
for the
Durango & Silverton
Narrow Gauge Railroad

Durango

160

0   5
Miles

N

LIST OF MAP SYMBOLS

D&SNG Railroad main line. Cross-ties are 1/10 mile apart.

Other D&SNG trackage.

Abandoned railroad.

Milepost, number of miles from Denver.

HERMOSA
el 6,645' (2,025 m)

Railroad station (not necessarily a building).

Water tank. Point of interest.

Major highway.

Street or road.

Trail or old toll road.

River.

Stream.

Intermittent stream.

Lake.

Molas Lake

Snowshed Slide

Major snowslide area.

Mount Eolus
14,083' (4,292 m)

Mountain peak.

Mount Garfield

U.S. Forest Service sign alongside track.

✕**9**

Mine or prospect. Numbered mines are named in text.

County boundary.

National Forest boundary.

Wilderness boundary.

Geologic contact between different rock formations.

Indistinct geologic contact.

Geologic fault.

Inferred fault.

Thrust fault.

Mineral vein.

Andesite and/or latite dike.

Mineralized dike.

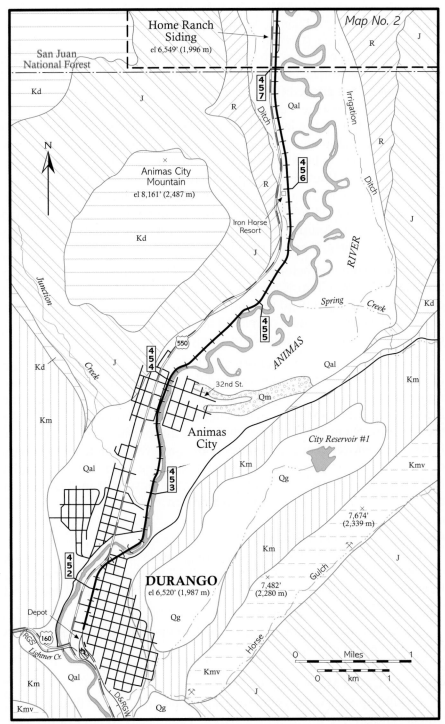

Home Ranch
Siding
el 6,549' (1,996 m)

San Juan
National Forest

R

J

Kd

J

R

457

Qal

Irrigation

R

N

Animas City
Mountain
el 8,161' (2,487 m)

456

R

J

Kd

R

Iron Horse
Resort

J

RIVER

Ditch

Junction

Spring

Creek

Kd

Kd

J

455

ANIMAS

Qal

Km

454

550

Creek

32nd St.

Qm

Km

Kd

J

Animas
City

City Reservoir #1

Km

Kmv

Km

Qal

453

Qg

Qg

×
7,674'
(2,339 m)

Kmv

Km

452

DURANGO
el 6,520' (1,987 m)

×
7,482'
(2,280 m)

Km

Gulch

J

Depot

Qg

RGS

160

Lightner Cr.

Qal

D&RGW

Km

Qg

Kmv

Horse

J

0   Miles   1

0   km   1

Mile

451.5 DURANGO DEPOT. MAP NO. 1, P. 11.

Elev. 6,520 ft (1,987 m)

Durango has been a railroad town since July 27, 1881, when the first D&RG construction train pulled into the new "town." Whistles, bells and a cheering crowd greeted the train at the site of the present depot. Even before track layers reached Durango, grading crews were working north toward Silverton on the last link of the D&RG Railway between Denver and the silver camp along the upper reaches of the Animas River. Only 45 miles were left to build, but what a challenge those miles proved to be! Yet, the Silverton Branch was completed in just 11 months. Men not working on the grade and track started building the depot, which was completed in January 1882. So today, as you leave on a memorable railroad journey along the Animas River, tip your hat to those undaunted builders of the 19th century. More on the history of Durango is on pp. 68-74.

About 30 minutes before the final call, a locomotive rolls off the ready track near the roundhouse, crosses College Drive (6th Street) north of the depot, and backs up toward the line of waiting coaches. A gentle (?) bump or two indicate the engine is coupled. The conductor gives the "All Aboard" call and your train starts northward along Narrow Gauge Avenue.

Each D&SNG train has a normal crew complement of five. In the cab of the locomotive are the engineer and fireman. The engineer sits on the right side of the cab (facing forward) and is in charge of operating the locomotive. The fireman sits on the left side of the cab and will hand stoke the fire throughout the day, shoveling three to four tons of coal into the firebox, one shovelful at a time. The conductor is responsible for the safety of the train and its passengers, and is assisted by a head brakeman and a rear brakeman. If you have any questions not answered in this book, a member of the crew will be happy to help you.

Milepost

452 CROSS 11TH STREET.

In the lively 1880s, Durango's sporting houses were west of the track on 10th and 11th Streets. The "shady ladies" houses had such names as Bessie's, Jennie's, Mattie's, the Variety Theater, Clipper, Silver Bell, and the Hanging Gardens of Babylon.

On the western skyline is Perins Peak, named for Charles Perin who surveyed the Durango townsite.

Mile

452.25 CROSS MAIN AVENUE.

Picking up speed, the engine whistles loud and clear at this crossing. Cinders and Smoke will become a part of your day as you follow the Mile by Mile Guide®.

452.4   CROSS ANIMAS RIVER.

This 253-ft bridge has been rebuilt several times. It consists of a steel plate girder span brought from the Pleasant Valley Branch in Utah in 1927, a steel Pratt truss span built in 1888 and brought from the Conejos River near Antonito, in 1917, and a wooden open-deck truss span built in 1936. The original bridge, built in 1881, was partially washed away during a spring flood in 1885.

A state fish hatchery, west of the track, is open to visitors every day. Started as a private hatchery, it was purchased by the state about 1900.

The houses to the east are on an outwash terrace (or plain) of loose gravel, sand, boulders, and soil deposited by meltwater streams flowing from a terminal moraine located almost two miles north (maps pp. 11 and 16). A terminal or end moraine is a mound or ridge that marks the farthest advance of a glacier. Behind the terrace is a cliff of soft gray-to-black Mancos Shale, which was deposited as mud in a sea some 90 million years ago.

A nice view of the La Plata Mountains is to the northwest. On the western skyline is another view of Perins Peak. It is capped with tan-to-rusty brown sandstone ledges of the Mesaverde Group that were deposited near the shore of an old sea. The Boston Coal & Fuel Co. opened a coal mine on the western side of Perins Peak in 1901. The Rio Grande Southern Railroad operated a privately-built branch to the mine and town which had a steady 4.5% grade and very sharp curves. The mine operated until 1926.

452.9   CROSS JUNCTION CREEK.

This stream flows into the Animas River from the northwest. The bridge was completely rebuilt during the winter of 1992.

453   TRACK ALONG ANIMAS RIVER.

Wildflowers include Rocky Mountain iris (photo, p. 93), sand lilies, tiny white daisies, and the ever-present dandelions in the spring; primroses, locoweed, sunflowers, and harebells in the summer months, and purple asters, yellow composites, and cattails in the fall.

453.9   CROSS 32ND STREET.

This is the site of Animas City, settled in 1874 (pp. 69,70). When the D&RG decided to follow the Animas River to Silverton, railroad officials proposed to build a depot and yards at Animas City if the town would cooperate by donating a right-of-way and depot site, help with grading through town and perhaps purchase railroad stock. Animas City declined the offer and the company town of Durango was laid out two miles below the struggling farming community. Grading was completed to Animas City

July 20, 1881, but track did not reach the town until October 1, 1881. Soon most businesses moved to Durango, and Animas City became a northern suburb. In 1947 the town was annexed to the city of Durango.

To the east are sinuous, low, hummocky hills of glacial debris that represent the signature of a terminal moraine. During Pleistocene time, starting about 10,000 years ago, the Animas Glacier, the largest in the San Juan Mountains, flowed as far south as Animas City. Here it stopped, deposited its load of sand, gravel, and boulders, and gradually receded to the high mountain cirques north and northwest of Silverton. These rounded irregular hills are best seen on the return trip.

Mile
454.7   TRAILER PARK.

The cliffs on the western skyline above the trailer park are thick, rusty-brown, and light tan layers of the Dakota Sandstone (Kd on map) at the top, which were deposited as sand in a sea about 100 million years ago. Below the Dakota Sandstone are multicolored shales, mudstones, and sandstones of the Morrison Formation, which were deposited as sand and mud by rivers and lakes about 150 million years ago. The base of the cliffs is massive, white-to-buff sandstone of the Entrada Formation, which was deposited by wind in ancient dunes about 160 million years ago. The Morrison and Entrada are shown together on maps as J.

As your train continues up the valley, the tilted sedimentary rocks gradually disappear beneath the surface. These same rocks are deeply buried in the San Juan Basin of northern New Mexico. Between Durango and Rockwood, the route passes sedimentary rocks that represent about 500 million years of geologic time (Geologic Column, pp. 84-85).

Milepost
455   SHARP BEND IN RIVER CHANNEL NEAR TRACK.

The Grand Motor Car and Piano Collection Museum is on the left. Established in 1992, the museum houses a fine collection of pianos and classic automobiles valued at more than $2 million. Open daily.

The buff-colored sandstone cliff above U.S. 550 and also across the valley is the Entrada Formation, included in unit J on Map No. 2 (p. 17). These rocks dip beneath the surface opposite mile 455.5. To the north are the first views of Permian and Upper Triassic redbeds (labeled R on maps).

Mile
455.9   UNITED CAMPGROUND.

This large campground is on the west side of the track.

After the 1989 fire that destroyed the original structure (pp. 113-116), the Durango roundhouse was expanded with eight new stalls. In 1998, these stalls were converted to a museum that displays railroad cars, locomotives, equipment, and memorabilia. This view shows the exterior fire-damaged wall of the original roundhouse used as a backdrop for photographs and railroad artifacts. Benches from both the Durango and Silverton depots sit on the former service pits.

(Becky Osterwald)

Milepost
456   IRON HORSE RESORT.

Along here you will see more nice views of the colorful sedimentary rocks. The bright red and rusty-red shales and thin sandstone layers are the Dolores Formation, which was deposited by rivers in an ancient desert about 170 to 187 million years ago. Animas City Mountain, elev. 8,170 ft (2,490 m), is on the western skyline.

Between mileposts 454 and 465, the Animas River meanders back and forth across the flat valley floor because the low stream gradient was established by the glacier. A number of cutoff meanders and oxbow lakes were formed when the river cut new, shorter channels between narrow, looping bends (photo, p. 24).

Thick willow groves are on both sides of the track. Shrubs along here include chokecherry, snowberry, buffaloberry, and box elder. In the late summer and fall, clematis vines have a fuzz of feathery seed tails hanging on the shrubs (photo, p. 92). These feathery seed plumes make excellent tinder as a spark from flint or pyrite struck into a ball of the fuzz will quickly ignite. Indians also used the seed plumes inside moccasins for padding and insulation.

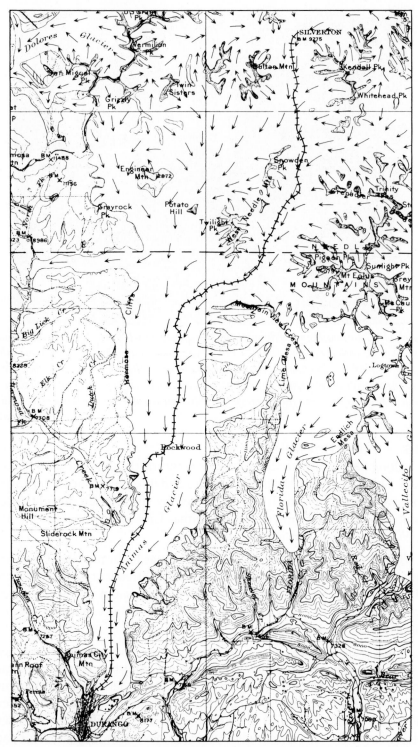

Maximum extent of the Wisconsin stage glaciers in the Animas Canyon area. After U.S. Geological Survey Professional Paper 166, plate 3.

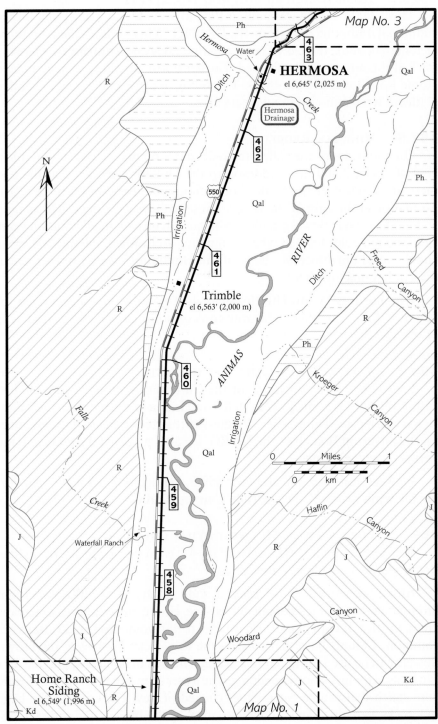

Ph

Hermosa

Water

HERMOSA
el 6,645' (2,025 m)

Qal

Ditch

Creek

Hermosa
Drainage

463

462

Ph

N

550

Qal

Ph

Irrigation

RIVER

461

Ditch

Freed

Canyon

Trimble
el 6,563' (2,000 m)

R

Ph

R

460

ANIMAS

Kroeger

Canyon

Falls

R

Irrigation

Qal

0   Miles   1

0   km   1

Creek

459

Haflin

Canyon

J

J

Waterfall Ranch

R

J

458

Canyon

Woodard

Home Ranch
Siding
el 6,549' (1,996 m)

R

Qal

J

Kd

Kd

Map No. 2

17

457.25   Home Ranch Siding. Map No. 2, p. 17

This 1,000-ft siding was built in 1982 to provide a meeting point for the additional trains that operate on the D&SNG. When rails reached this point October 20, 1881, the D&RG construction crews never dreamed a passing track at this site would be needed. Farther north, an old spur track named Home Ranch was at mile 457.9. The siding, a cattle chute, and a wooden platform were removed many years ago.

457.5   Views of Redbeds.

On both sides of the valley, the redbeds (R on maps) have a total thickness of about 2,500 ft. In addition to the Dolores Formation at the top, there are 1,900 ft of the Cutler Formation, and about 130 ft of the Rico Formation at the base of the valley. These redbeds were deposited as sand and mud by rivers flowing across an ancient desert about 200 million years ago. The red color formed when magnetite, an iron-bearing mineral, rusts and the resulting minerals—hematite and limonite—coated and cemented the sand grains together.

Due north is Potato Hill (locally called Spud Mountain), named for "Potato" John Raymond, a favorite cook on some early geological surveys of the West.

458.5   Waterfall on Cliff to the West.

Falls Creek flows off layers of the Cutler Formation. The ranch, just east of the falls, is named "Waterfall," and is one of the oldest in the valley. It was started by Thomas H. Wigglesworth, chief construction engineer for the Silverton Branch of the D&RG. He also surveyed the branch to the Perins Peak coal mine.

Between milepost 458 and mile 459.5, herds of elk often are seen during the winter runs of the **Cascade Canyon Train**.

459   First View of Mountain View Crest.

This mountain range (Map No. 5, p. 44) is on the northeastern skyline. Better views are farther up the canyon.

Along both sides of the track, a wide variety of wildflowers bloom throughout the summer and fall. Silver sage, clover, butter and eggs, clematis vines, thistles, Indian paintbrush (photo, p. 93), goldenrod, and cattails are common. Cattails have many uses—the leaves can be woven, the brown flowers can be used for tinder in starting a fire, or in bouquets, and the fuzz can be used for insulation or bedding. The lower stem and roots contain nearly pure starch that can be eaten either cooked or raw. The cores of the large rootstocks were dried and ground into meal by the Indians and early settlers. Muskrat, geese, and elk like to feed on the rootstocks and new shoots.

Hermosa House Hotel at Trimble Hot Springs circa 1910. This peaceful scene was recorded by D&RG photographer, George L. Beam.

(D&RGW collection, courtesy Jackson C. Thode)

Mile

460.7   TRIMBLE HOT SPRINGS.

Elev. 6,563 ft (2,000 m)

A small depot with a platform was built in 1883 for excursionists who came from Durango and other towns. There was also a short siding.

William and Rufina Trimble settled near the springs in 1874. William found that the curative hot water helped his rheumatism, so in March 1882, he purchased 160 acres of land surrounding the springs for $200 and planned to build a spa. Because the Trimbles were having financial problems, the property was sold to entrepreneur T.D. Burns of Tierra Amarilla, New Mexico. The Burns family completed the first hotel and spa, which opened December 28, 1882, with a grand ball. A post office opened January 29, 1883, and lasted until September 1900.

In 1892, the first Trimble Hot Springs Hotel was destroyed by fire. The Burns family replaced the first hotel with the lavish Hermosa House Hotel in 1896. This structure lasted until July 30, 1931, when it also burned to the ground. With a change of ownership in the 1930s, a two-story pink stucco and glass-block building with a dining room and ballroom were built on the site of Hermosa House. A third fire destroyed the main building in 1963, and the resort was closed until 1988, when facilities for bath-

19

ing were rebuilt by new owners. Remarkably, the water flowing from the base of the cliff still averages 120 gallons per minute at an average temperature of 111°F.

Milepost
462   VIEWS OF ANIMAS VALLEY.

The Animas Valley from Durango to Baker's Bridge, east of milepost 466, is a broad U-shape in which the river meanders back and forth in wide sweeping curves.

Among the many wildflowers, watch for mullein, a 2-4 ft tall, coarse, woolly, spiked plant with small yellow flowers (photo, p. 92). It blooms in July. The large, coarse, olive-green leaves are velvet-like to touch, and contain chemicals used in lotions to soften the skin and in medicine to soothe inflamed tissues. Small birds eat the seeds in the dried, brown spikes when other food is covered with snow. The plant was brought to this country from Europe.

Mile
462.45   CROSS HERMOSA CREEK.

The bridge is a 64-ft long wooden Howe pony truss, installed in 1914.

Mile
462.5   HERMOSA.
Elev. 6,645 ft (2,025 m)

A passing track and water tank are here. Locomotives are watered from a tank car body. The D&SNG keeps its maintenance-of-way equipment at this site. A wye, a frame depot and platform, section house, bunkhouse, and coal house were here many years ago. Hermosa's first settlers arrived in 1873-74. A post office was established July 27, 1876, and lasted until September 1900. Mail came via Howardsville, Silverton, and down the

Listen for one long whistle blast from the locomotive, indicating that your train is approaching Hermosa. Whenever the train approaches a designated station or flagstop, the engineer will blow one long whistle. He then will look back for instructions from the train crew, usually the head brakeman standing on the rear platform of the first coach. The brakeman will signal the engineer with either a "highball" or a "stop" (diagram, p. 118). A highball is a high, semicircular wave of the hand, indicating to the engineer that the train should proceed through the station without stopping. When the engineer observes a highball, he responds with two short blasts of the whistle. If the conductor wishes to stop the train, he will have the head brakeman signal a "stop," which is a low, swinging motion of his hand. When the engineer observes this signal, he responds with three short blasts of the whistle instead, and then brings the train to a stop. This whistle signal of one long and three short blasts is also the indication for the rear-end brakeman to grab his flagging kit and prepare to protect the rear of the train while it is stopped. Also note the list of whistle signals on the inside front cover.

Two views of Hermosa circa 1905-1906. The scene at the top looks northwest toward Hermosa Mountain. The bottom view looks south and shows the depot, bunkhouse, and section foreman s house. The siding at left probably has some original 30-lb rail in place, while the mainline has at least a vestige of ballast between the ties.

(W.R. Self, Center for Southwest Studies, Ft. Lewis College)

21

Animas Canyon, on the Animas Canyon Toll Road that was built in 1876-77. See pp. 68 and 74 for more history of the toll road. A railroad construction camp was located here after construction started from Durango. Track reached Hermosa November 1, 1881.

One of the early journalists to describe the wonders of the Silverton Branch was Ernest Ingersoll (1852-1946), who wrote for the New York *Tribune, Harper s Magazine,* and *Scribner s Monthly.* He first visited the San Juans in 1874 as a recorder for the Hayden Survey and wrote a book, *Knocking Round the Rockies,* which described his early adventures with the survey. During the early 1880s, Ingersoll and his wife returned to Colorado, and with the blessing of S.K. Hooper, general passenger agent of the D&RG, the couple traveled on all the D&RG narrow gauge lines. A book, *Crest of the Continent,* resulted from those travels. Ingersoll described the Animas Canyon as "The Queen of the Cañons." Prior to that extensive trip, he came to Colorado in 1882 and described the construction of the Silverton Branch in the April 1882 issue of *Harper s Magazine:*

> ...Through the bottom we could see, running straight as an arrow, the graded bed of the coming railroad, but the stage-road kept away from it until we reached the few cabins that constitute Hermosa.
>
> Presently we came upon one of Mr. Wigglesworth's construction camps—long, low buildings of logs with dirt roofs, where grasses and sunflowers and purple asters make haste to sprout, are grouped without order. Perhaps there will also be an immense tent where the crew eats. Beside the larger houses, inhabited by the engineers, foremen, etc., you will see numbers of little huts about three logs high, roofed flatly with poles, brush, and mud, and having only a window-like hole to creep in and out through; or into a sidehill will be pushed small caves with a front wall of stones or mud and a bit of canvas for a door—in these kennels the laboring men find shelter.

This is the only description of a construction camp that was found during research for this book. According to Robert W. Richardson, founder of the Colorado Railroad Museum at Golden, few construction photographs exist of early-day mountain railroads in Colorado. He believes that the builders probably did not want prospective investors and stockholders to see the terrain and methods used to build these lines, because to Easterners, the mountain construction must have seemed almost impossible. After a section of track was completed, photographers were welcome to publicize the accomplishments.

Mile
462.7   TRACK CROSSES U.S. 550.

After crossing the highway, the grade abruptly changes from 1.2% to a steady 2.5% all the way to Rockwood. Your locomotive will begin working at full throttle for the next six miles, known to D&SNG railroaders as "Hermosa Hill." Watch out—here come the cinders! The track climbs along the west side of the valley to bypass the box canyon of the Animas above Baker's Bridge. For the next two miles, the track winds along the slope in curves that range from 12° to 24°.

Milepost
463   NICE VIEW ACROSS VALLEY. MAP NO. 3, P. 25.

Excellent morning photos of the lovely Animas Valley are possible along here. There are many marvelous vistas of the placid, meandering Animas River for the next several miles.

The brown, tan, and gray cliffs along the track are part of the limestone, shale and sandstone layers of the Hermosa Group (Ph on maps), about 650 ft thick. These sedimentary rocks were deposited as limy mud in a sea about 270 million years ago.

The train is climbing into the timbered hills of the Piñon-Juniper Life Zone. Mullein and yucca (photo, p. 92) are plentiful. The Indians made soap from yucca by pounding and pulverizing the roots. Trees along the track include low-growing dwarf junipers, Rocky Mountain junipers, some quite large Gambel (scrub) oaks, and widely spaced ponderosa pines.

Mile
463.8   HONEYVILLE FARM BELOW TRACK.

When you see the Honeyville sign, look for the beekeeper's hut on the east side of the track. The hives and processing plant are open to visitors.

Mile
464.5   MISSIONARY RIDGE ACROSS VALLEY.

A logging road across the valley switches back and forth to the top of Missionary Ridge. This ridge was named by an army unit stationed in the valley in the 1870s that had fought on Missionary Ridge near Chattanooga, Tennessee, during the Civil War and had noticed a similarity of the two skylines.

Milepost
465   PROMINENT GRAY TO BROWN LEDGE.

Across the valley, at the base of a cliff, is a prominent ledge of Cambrian Ignacio Quartzite (Ci on the map). It was deposited as sand brought to an ancient sea by rivers between 500 and 525 million years ago. The Ignacio Quartzite is the oldest sedimentary unit in the Animas Valley.

Mile
465.75   PINKERTON SIDING.

This 700-ft siding was built in 1982 as a passing track for the additional trains that now are operated by the D&SNG. For several years the westbound **Cascade Canyon Train**, Number 265, met the eastbound **Second Silverton Train**, Number 464, in the late afternoon. (You may wonder why your train, which is headed north, is referred to as the "westbound" train. This term goes back to the days of D&RG ownership, when the San Juan Extension was headed *west* from Alamosa.)

On May 24, 1981, the second day of operations for the new D&SNG Railroad, this double-headed train starts to climb the 2.5 percent grade to Rockwood after passing Hermosa and crossing U.S. 550. (F.W. Osterwald)

View northward of the Animas River valley from Animas City Mountain. Trimble Hot Springs is in the distance near the base of the western cliffs, and Hermosa is at the base of Hermosa Mountain on the left skyline. The river meanders back and forth across the flat valley floor. A number of cut-off meanders, termed ox-bow lakes, are in the foreground.
(F. Gonner, Center for Southwest Studies, Ft. Lewis College)

24

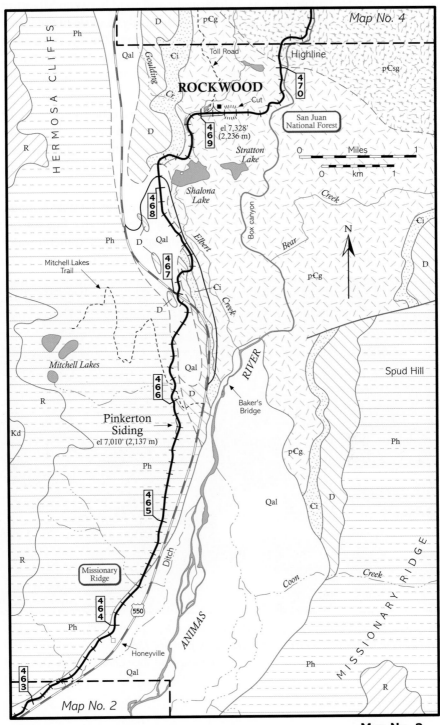

HERMOSA CLIFFS

Ph

Qal

D

pCg

Toll Road

Goulding

Ci

Highline

4 7 0

pCsg

ROCKWOOD

Cut

San Juan
National Forest

Ci

4 6 9
el 7,328'
(2,236 m)

Stratton
Lake

0   Miles   1

0   km   1

Shalona
Lake

Creek

D

4 6 8

Bear

Ci

Ph

D

Qal

Elbert

Box canyon

N

D

Mitchell Lakes
Trail

4 6 7

pCg

D

Ci
Creek

D

Mitchell Lakes

Qal

Spud Hill

R

4 6 6

RIVER

Ph

D

Kd

Baker's
Bridge

**Pinkerton
Siding**
el 7,010' (2,137 m)

Ph

pCg

4 6 5

Qal

Ci

D

R

Ditch

Missionary
Ridge

Coon

Creek

MISSIONARY RIDGE

4 6 4

550

ANIMAS

Ph

Ph

Honeyville

4 6 3

Qal

R

Map No. 2

Map No. 3

The siding is named for Judge J.H. Pinkerton, whose ranch included some hot springs. The ranch was a stop on the toll road between Silverton and Animas City. The Pinkertons were the fifth family to settle in the lower Animas valley. In August 1880, the famous Ute Chief, Ouray, stopped at the Pinkerton ranch for two days. He was ill, but continued on to Ignacio, where he died August 24, 1880. The Indians buried him near Ignacio, but kept the location a secret for 45 years.

Years later, the Pinkerton ranch became a guest ranch known as El Rancho Encantado. The property changed hands and became Pinkerton Hot Springs, and during the 1960s, the name was changed to the Golden Horseshoe Resort. Today the buildings, well below the tracks and the highway, house the Timberline Academy, a private school.

The hot springs on the property are very similar to the Trimble Springs, but the water is not as hot. The rusty, yellow-brown deposits that line the hill down to the river are travertine, deposited by the springs. The mineral water emerges along small faults that probably are parallel to the Hermosa Cliffs.

The Durango Wheel Club s excursion to Baker s Bridge, June 16, 1895. This is undoubtedly a replacement for the first bridge built by the Baker party in 1860-61.

(F. Gonner, Pear Tree Camera Shop, Durango)

HISTORIC BAKER'S BRIDGE.

Look upstream to the north. This is the site of the first settlement in the Animas Valley. A group of prospectors, led by Captain Charles Baker (pp. 68-69), spent the winter of 1860-61 in a cabin they built along the river. The Baker party also built the first crude log bridge across the Animas River at this location. In the years following, a few other cabins were built along the river, and the area was known as Elbert, the First Animas City, Old Animas City, or Animas City 1. A toll gate for the Animas Canyon Toll Road also was located at this site.

Milepost
466   CLIFFS ABOVE TRACK.

Brown and rusty gray limestone cliffs of the Hermosa Group are easy to see at this milepost. Gambel oaks are on both sides of the track. The shiny dark green leaves turn a lovely bronze and reddish color in the fall.

Mile
466.1   MITCHELL LAKES TRAIL CROSSING.

A popular trail for hikers and horseback riders crosses the track and heads up the hill to several small lakes (Map No. 3, p. 25). Listen for the warning whistle. A KOA Campground is below the highway.

Ponderosa pine is the dominant tree. It has a reddish-brown bark and may grow to 150 ft.

Milepost
467   U.S. 550 HIGHWAY OVERPASS.

This overpass was built in the late 1970s so the highway could avoid the steep grade and sharp curves near Shalona Lake. The overpass is a popular stop for rail photographers.

Between miles 466.8 and 467.8, the speed limit is 10 mph because of the many sharp curves. D&SNG railroaders call the track above the county road the "Mini High Line." These cliffs are Ouray Limestone (D on Map No. 3), which are composed of small shell fragments deposited in sea water about 330 million years ago.

Mile
467.3   VIEW OF ENGINEER MOUNTAIN.

Standing at an elevation of 12,972 ft (3,954 m), this pyramid-shaped peak is on the northern skyline. Along County Road 250, below the track and across the river, are Precambrian granite outcrops that were rounded and polished by the Animas Glacier as it slowly moved down the valley. Notice how the Ignacio Quartzite lies on the granite.

The sound of the engine as it labors up the 2.5% grade should now be very familiar. On the return trip, the coaches swing and sway along these curves and lull passengers into a drowsy state of relaxation.

Rabbitbrush shrubs.

Typical Montane forest between Shalona Lake and Rockwood. Bright green, low-growing, shrub-like trees are scrub oak. Taller, olive-green trees are junipers and at the top of the hill are dark-green ponderosa pines.　　　　　　*(Both photos D.B. Osterwald)*

467.8   OPEN HILLSIDE.

Just before crossing county road 250 (old U.S. 550), notice the lovely sloping hillside covered with rabbitbrush (photo, p. 28) and sweetbriar roses. The 3-4 ft high rabbitbrush shrubs along the track have olive-green leaves and gray branches. In the fall the shrubs are a mass of beautiful yellow blossoms.

Mile
468.1   TRACK CROSSES COUNTY HIGHWAY.

Picturesque Shalona Lake is to the east. This lake is fed by Elbert Creek, named for Samuel H. Elbert, a San Juan pioneer and Colorado Territorial governor in 1873-74.

A short distance north of the highway crossing, Bell Spur and Rockwood Quarry were on the west side of the track years ago. The quarry was owned and operated by John F. Bell, who shipped limestone to a Durango smelter for use as flux.

Mile
468.5   SITE OF TRAIN WRECK.

On January 21, 1917, a special eastbound train turned over as it rounded a sharp curve, known locally as Granite Point. The newspapers of the day referred to this accident as the "Millionaire Special" because several prominent businessmen interested in purchasing the famous Sunnyside Mine (pp. 80-81) near Silverton were on board. Remarkably, none of the 20 passengers were seriously injured, but a fire destroyed two of the three coaches on the train when a coal stove overturned. A 10 mph slow order is required at this sharp curve.

On May 26, 1981, the first narrow gauge stock extra in many years is ready to leave Rockwood with horses for Ah! Wilderness Guest Ranch. Several cars of pipe, timbers and other material for the Tacoma power plant are on the siding waiting to be moved.   (F.W. Osterwald)

*Rockwood, Colorado in 1885. Train Number 51, the **Accomodation**, with an unidentified locomotive, is standing at the depot. Narrow gauge boxcar 3790 is sitting on the north leg of the wye. The tree stumps in the forground are in an area that was surveyed for town lots but never developed.*

(Nathan Boyce, by permission of the Colorado Railroad Museum, Golden, Colorado)

CAMBRIAN-PRECAMBRIAN CONTACT.

This major contact (boundary) between the light-colored Cambrian Ignacio Quartzite (€i) and red coarse-grained Precambrian granite (p€g) is easy to see along the left side of the train, especially when the morning sun reflects off the mineral grains. The granite probably cooled from its molten state about 1.5 billion years ago.

Just beyond this contact the track makes a sharp (24°) curve and enters a small canyon along Elbert Creek. Between Hermosa and Rockwood the track has a maximum curvature of 24° (see p. 122) and a maximum grade of 2.5% in climbing 722 ft between the two points.

Wildflowers include yucca, sumac, box elder, chokecherry, rabbitbrush, wild rose, mullein, and scarlet gilia. Many cattails line Elbert Creek.

Mile
468.9 PRIVATE POND ON WEST.

This property would be a great place to live and watch trains during the busy summer months.

469.1   ROCKWOOD.
Elev. 7,367 ft (2,245 m)

A 750-ft siding and wye are located at this flag stop. A train will not stop here unless directed to by the conductor. The tail of the wye, a track shaped like the letter Y, and used for reversing the direction of trains, has an ancient stub switch, probably the last one in use anywhere in the United States. Beyond Rockwood, there are no roads. The only access to the Animas Canyon from here to Silverton is on the train, on foot, or on horseback.

A post office was established July 8, 1876, and except for several intermittent closings, lasted until February 15, 1940. Grading and bridging crews reached Rockwood in September 1881, but track-laying was not completed until November 26, 1881. Passenger service between Durango and Rockwood commenced in January 1882. It is difficult to believe that for a decade this location was a bustling town. During 1882, a depot, platform, section house, bunkhouse, and coal house were built. Rockwood was a popular holiday destination for picnickers from Durango and Animas City. Round trip fare was $2. See page 74 for more on the history of Rockwood (photo, p. 75).

469.2   ENTER ROCKWOOD CUT.

In 1955, this famous 350-ft cut was covered and made into a tunnel for the movie, "Around the World in 80 Days." The cut has been a favorite place for photographs since the Silverton Branch was completed.

The only *downgrade* stretch of track on the entire westbound trip to Silverton is from the northern end of Rockwood Cut to the high bridge at mile 471.2.

469.4   SAN JUAN NATIONAL FOREST SIGN.

Beside the track is an automatic wheel-flange oiler which was installed in 1981. This device reduces wear on the rail and wheel flanges.

469.5   HIGH LINE.

Have your camera ready for the spectacular views as the train snakes along the narrow shelf blasted out of red granite. The engineer has a permanent "slow order" through this gorge for safety, but also for the benefit of photographers. The water in this box canyon is more than 400 ft below the track. Wheel flanges squeak and groan, adding sound effects that are difficult to forget. Several scenes from "Butch Cassidy and the Sundance Kid" were filmed along here in 1968.

The High Line was the most difficult portion of the Silverton Branch to build. To drill into the granite walls and set the black powder shots, men had to be lowered on ropes from above. It cost about $100,000 per mile to build this narrow shelf during the late winter and early spring of 1882.

*Engine 481 with the **Silverton Mixed** on the High Line, October 15, 1981.   (F.W. Osterwald)*

On July 23, 1982, Silverton bound Train number 461 slowly rounds the first sharp curve along the High Line. The Cinco Animas private car (p. 154) is on the rear of the train.

(F.W. Osterwald and J.B. Bennetti, Jr.)

In 1903 or 1904, Monte Ballough recorded this dramatic view of the High Line above the Animas River with the large curved trestle at mile 470.2 in the background, shortly before the trestle burned. It was replaced with a fill. Grand View Park, on the slopes above the trestle, was a popular picnic spot for excursionists who rode special trains to Rockwood. The section men at the left are on a handcar that was propelled manually by pumping the handles up and down. (Rieke's Photo Arts Studio, Durango)

On December 27, 1921, this mixed train traveling to Durango hit a rock slide south of Tacoma. The head engine, 270, jumped the track, taking the flanger and engine 263 with it into the river. Fireman Hindelang jumped from the train and was not hurt, but engineer Louis Johnson was injured, and fireman John Connor was crushed to death beneath the wreckage. Both engines were repaired and remained in service many more years.

(Monte Ballough, Colorado Historical Society)

470   **U**PPER **E**ND OF **S**HELF **T**RACK.

At track level, the Central Claim was discovered in 1882. A shear fault here contains a little gold and silver in hematite-chalcopyrite quartz veins. Another series of faults are along the contact (or boundary) between red granite (pꞒg) and metamorphosed schists and gneisses (pꞒsg). The schists and gneisses were changed (metamorphosed) from older igneous or sedimentary rocks by extreme heat and pressure as much as 2.5 billion years ago.

Scenes from "Night Passage" and "Denver & Rio Grande" were filmed along this portion of the line.

In the fall, tall tansy asters and goldenrod are abundant along the track. Tall ponderosa pines and junipers are plentiful along both sides of the valley.

Between mile 470.3 and 470.4 there was a long wooden trestle that burned in 1905. Today this area is called Overland Curve by D&SNG railroaders (photo, p. 33).

Mile
471.2   **C**ROSS **A**NIMAS **R**IVER **(M**AP **N**O. **4, P. 37).**

The bridge is a 130-ft wrought-iron deck-truss bridge which was built in 1880 but not installed until 1894. It was strengthened in 1981 so the heavier 480- and 490-series locomotives can safely cross the bridge.

Mile
471.3   **S**ITE OF **T**RAIN **W**RECK.

Photographs of this accident are on page 34. Evidence of the ramp that was cut into the hillside and used to drag the wrecked engines back to track level still is visible on the west side above the river.

The river has cut down into the granite at places of least resistance (mostly along joints and fractures in the rock) to form a narrow, postglacial gorge. For the next six miles, the track is built on highly metamorphosed gneisses and schists.

Scrub oak is still very abundant, but firs are beginning to be seen and river willows are common.

Mile
471.7   **S**ITE OF **S**AVAGE.

A short spur track on the east was removed many years ago.

Mile
472.05   **C**ANYON **C**REEK. **C**RAZY **W**OMAN **C**REEK **S**IGN.

Track crosses Canyon Creek. Crazy Woman Creek is actually a tributary of Canyon Creek.

***The Silverton**, pulled by engine 481, crosses the high bridge below Tacoma. The blow-off cocks are open to clean out the lower portions of the boiler.*   *(Kenneth T. Gustafson)*

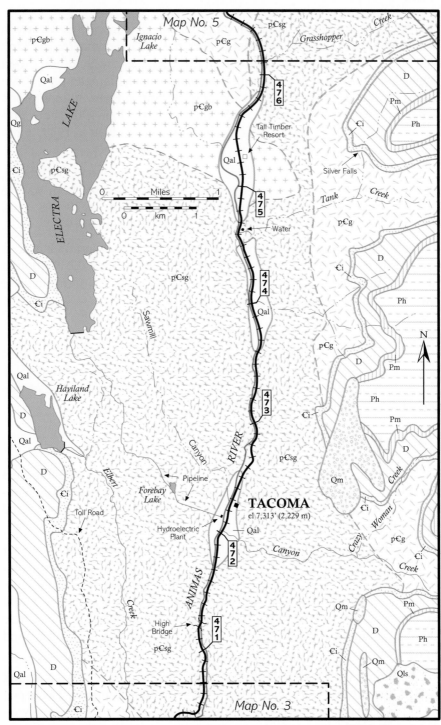

Ignacio
Lake

Grasshopper

Creek

p€gb

Qal

p€sg

p€g

p€gb

476

D

Pm

Ci

Ph

Tall Timber
Resort

Qal

Silver Falls

Qg

Ci

p€sg

Tank

Creek

475

ELECTRA

LAKE

Water

p€g

D

Miles

Ci

D

Ci

km

p€sg

474

D

Ph

Qal

Sawmill

Pm

p€g

N

Haviland
Lake

Qal

473

D

Ph

D

RIVER

Ci

Pm

Qal

Canyon

p€sg

D

Elbert

Pipeline

Qm

Forebay
Lake

TACOMA

el 7,313' (2,229 m)

Ci

Woman

Crazy

Toll Road

Hydroelectric
Plant

Qal

p€g

Ci

Ci

D

ANIMAS

472

Canyon

Creek

Creek

Qm

Pm

High
Bridge

471

D

Ph

Ci

Qm

Creek

p€sg

Qls

Qal

D

Ci

472.3   Tacoma.
Elev. 7,313 ft (2,229 m)

This is a flag stop. Across the river is the oldest hydroelectric facility in the U.S. that still uses its original generators, the 1905 Tacoma Power Plant. Water to turn the generators comes from Electra Lake, a reservoir on Elbert Creek, 934 ft above the power plant, through a 66-inch diameter pipe. From Forebay Lake, water descends to the power plant in three 30-inch pipes. Generator 2 was completed in 1905, and generator 1 in 1906; both produce two megawatts of power. A third generator was added in 1949, and it produces four megawatts of power.

A spur track to the power plant was washed out in the flood of October 5, 1911, when heavy rains widened the river channel at Tacoma from 90 ft to 170 ft. Twenty-two miles of track were destroyed (photos, pp. 39, 108, 110). The retaining walls were built after another flood in September 1970.

During the spring, when the Animas River is high, rafters and kayakers who test their skills on an exciting ride down the river catch the eastbound train for Durango at Tacoma. Attempting a ride farther south through the Animas Canyon Gorge is foolhardy, to say the least.

Milepost
473   Metamorphic Rock Along Track.
For the next mile are outcrops of dark gray, layered gneiss with intruded masses of igneous diabase, gray granite, and some white quartz veins (pЄsg). Diabase is a fine-grained, dark-gray-to-black igneous rock composed of plagioclase feldspar and pyroxene. It often is used for tombstones.

Milepost
474   Cabins of Former Guest Ranch.
Elev. 7,473 ft (2,278 m)

For 33 years (1952-1985) this was a well-known resort, Ah! Wilderness Guest Ranch. The buildings are used now to house the staff for Tall Timber Resort, located at mile 475.25. A five-car spur track on the east is used to store freight for Tall Timber Resort.

The buildings stand in a fairly flat valley, or park. The Animas Glacier gouged out a narrow trough which later was filled partly with stream alluvium, a general term for unconsolidated materials deposited during Quaternary (or recent) time. In the fall, when the level of the river is low, round depressions or potholes in the rocks of the stream channel are visible. These potholes gradually were formed by water whirling stones and gravel around in one spot.

Wildflowers grow abundantly in this open park. Only a few scrub oak grow at this elevation, but aspen trees are becoming common. The aspen has a gray-green to white bark and round green leaves that are nearly always moving, which gives it the name "quaking aspen" or "quakie."

The October 5, 1911, Animas River flood washed out a spur track and bridge to the power plant at Tacoma. At the height of the flood, the river channel increased from 90 to 170 feet wide. *(Colorado Historical Society)*

Fifty-nine years later, a similar scene near Tacoma caused by too much water in the Animas River. September 10, 1970. *(R. W. Osterwald)*

From the east side of the train, look northwestward to the cliffs above the valley. If you are lucky, you may catch a quick glimpse of SILVER FALLS shimmering in the sun as the water tumbles down a cliff of the Ignacio Quartzite (Map No. 4, p. 37). The trees have grown so much in recent years the falls are difficult to see.

Mile
474.6   TANK CREEK WATER TANK.
         Elev. 7,462 ft (2,274 m)
Westbound trains stop here to take water stored in a steel tank car body mounted on concrete supports. While just as efficient as the original wooden water tank, it is hardly as attractive. The original wooden tank was removed in November 1966.

During this and at other stops, you may notice the crew getting off the train. At the appropriate whistle signal (see inside front cover), the rear brakeman will walk down the track beyond the end of the train a prescribed distance to warn any oncoming trains or railroad "speeders" (track cars) that a train is stopped ahead. The head brakeman and conductor may use the opportunity to perform a brief visual inspection of the brake rigging and wheel assemblies under the coaches. Listen for another whistle signal from the engineer to call for the flagman to return just before the train is ready to move.

The track crosses Tank Creek, a roaring mountain stream that originates on the southern slope of Mountain View Crest, just before it enters the river at the water tank. This train stop affords a good opportunity to see how the river has cut through the gneiss and schist along joints and fractures. Lateral moraines are on both sides of the Animas in this portion of the canyon.

Water birch is common along the river and at the mouth of Tank Creek. This slender-stemmed tree with a shiny, dark bronze-to-copper bark grows to about 25 ft tall.

Mile
475.25   TALL TIMBER RESORT.
The small depot is a reception building for guests arriving or departing this secluded, five-star luxury resort. The only other access to Tall Timber is by helicopter. This open valley with lush aspen groves is a prime location for wildflowers. The Colorado state flower, the blue columbine, thrives in moist, shady aspen groves (photos, p. 55, 93). It is found at elevations between 6,000 ft (1,800 m) and 11,000 ft (3,300 m) and blooms from late June in the lower elevations till mid-August higher in the mountains.

Several movies were filmed in this small park. A replica of an 1880 town was built here for the movie, "Denver and Rio Grande." The climax of this epic was the intentional head-on collision and destruction of two of

On July 17, 1951, an intentional head-on collision of D&RGW engines 319 and 345 was filmed on the Silverton Branch for the movie, "Denver and Rio Grande." The scene was set in the open park at milepost 475, at what is now Tall Timber Resort. Engine 345, on the right, was renumbered 268 for the movie. Both engines were ruined in the collision and were dismantled in the fall of 1951.   *(Center for Southwest Studies, Ft. Lewis College)*

the railroad's locomotives. At the time (1951), the D&RGW management viewed the narrow gauge as an obsolete misfit suitable only for junking.

Parts of "Night Passage," "Ticket to Tomahawk" (photo, p. 66), "Naked Spur," and "Around the World in 80 Days" also were filmed along the Silverton Branch. A number of other movies have been filmed at other sites in the San Juans, including "Colorado Territory," "Across the Wide Missouri," "Viva Zapata," "Three Young Texans," "Run for Cover," "Maverick Queen," "Butch Cassidy and the Sundance Kid," "Support your Local Gunfighter," and "The Tracker." During the fall of 1994, a sequel to Ken Burns' documentary on the Civil War, entitled "The West," was filmed on the Silverton Branch using the tiny *Eureka* locomotive (pp. 160-161).

Although the track is on Quaternary alluvium deposits, Precambrian gabbro (p€gb) crops out on both sides of the valley between milepost 475 and mile 475.6. Gabbro is a dark-colored, equigranular igneous rock that was injected as a hot fluid into the older gneisses and schists, probably about 2 billion years ago. Boundaries between the different types of igneous rocks commonly are irregular and indefinite.

476.1   Cross Grasshopper Creek.

The bridge was completely rebuilt during the winter of 1993-94. Cement trucks were hauled to the site on flatcars to pour the footings.

This stream begins on the southern slopes Mountain View Crest. An alluvial fan is at the mouth of the creek.

476.7   Little Cascade Creek (Map No. 5, p. 44).

This stream joins the Animas River on the west. A concrete retaining wall was built after the 1970 flood.

477   Enter Small Open Park.

Small rock slides are along the east side of the valley. Columbines are abundant here in July.

477.5   Cascade Canyon Wye.
Elev. 7,696 ft (2,346 m)

This wye, built in 1981, is used to turn the **Cascade Canyon Winter Train** and other special excursions. On August 14, 1999, a new 2400 sq. ft covered pavilion with a fireplace was dedicated as Cascade Station. The facility is used for lunch service during the winter and in the summer for private parties and events in conjunction with charter train operations.

Cascade Canyon enters the Animas River from the northwest, a short distance north of the wye. This narrow canyon opens up into a small park-like area called Purgatory Flats which is about three miles northwest of the mouth of Cascade Creek. In this flat, Purgatory Creek and Lime Creek join Cascade Creek. How the name "Purgatory" evolved is not known, but one version suggests that the narrow, steep-walled section of Cascade Creek is called Purgatory because it is hard to get in and hard to get out!

The winter of 1878-79 was one of the mildest on record all over the West. In April 1879, fires started at a number of places in the mountains to the west and northwest, and did not burn themselves out until the following September. By June, Cascade Creek Canyon and Purgatory Flats were at the center of an ever-expanding wall of flames. Throughout the summer, fires raged along Lime Creek, extending as far north as the Molas Mine, located on the hill above mile 493.3. More than 26,000 acres of timber were burned, much of it on the east side of U.S. 550. Silverton escaped, but suffocating smoke filled Baker's Park for many weeks.

As the train continues to climb, the coniferous forest is beginning to change. Subtle differences in color and shape of the spruces, firs, and pines can make identification of the different species from the moving train difficult, although Colorado Blue Spruces are easy to spot because of their beautiful tapered shape and silvery blue-green needles. Closer to Silverton Engelmann spruce and limber pines are more common.

Mile
477.75 TEFFT FLAG STOP.

The original location of Tefft was at 477.9. The D&SNG moved the stop to this point to allow easier loading and unloading of passengers and freight.

Mile
477.8 CROSSES ANIMAS RIVER.

The north span of this wrought-iron bridge was built in 1887 and placed here in 1911. The south steel span was built in 1972. The Needle Mountains are on the skyline to the northeast.

Mile
477.9 ORIGINAL LOCATION OF TEFFT.
Elev. 7,712 ft (2,351 m)

This station is named for Guy Tefft, an early-day forest ranger. It is also the location of Niccora, a short-lived way station on the toll road started by Frank E. Blackledge, who also petitioned for a post office. The post office operated from July 16, 1877, to November 26, 1877, when Blackledge, the postmaster, left for the winter and never returned. During 1878, Thomas Charlton briefly considered building a hotel at the site of Blackledge's cabins. A cabin standing on the north side of Cascade Creek is probably on the site of Niccora. This cabin, built in 1941, is owned by Ernie Schaaf of Durango.

A large sawmill, built in the 1890s and operated by the Matevie brothers, was located here. It produced mine timbers and railroad ties for the Silverton Northern RR (see p. 80) as well as the D&RG. Timber was cut from spruce-fir forests along Cascade and Lime Creeks and floated to the mill. Remains of the locomotive boiler from the Silverton Northern engine *Gold King* are almost completely hidden from view on the hillside northwest of this point.

The Animas Canyon Toll Road from Silverton to Animas City was along the west side of the Animas River to Tefft. The grade is now very difficult to find and, in many places, the railroad was built on the old road. At Tefft, the road crossed Cascade Creek and climbed the rather open Cascade Hill to the west in a series of three switchbacks. It took six horses to pull the stages to the top of Cascade Hill where another way station, operated by homesteader Sam Smith, was located. From the top, the toll road crossed Little Cascade Creek and continued south along Elbert Creek, passing Rockwood, Pinkerton's ranch, and Hermosa, following in a general way the present route of U.S. 550 highway. There were toll gates at Baker's Bridge, (Map No. 3, p. 25) and in the canyon below Silverton. The fare was $6 one way. Additional details about the toll road are on pp. 22, 74, 76.

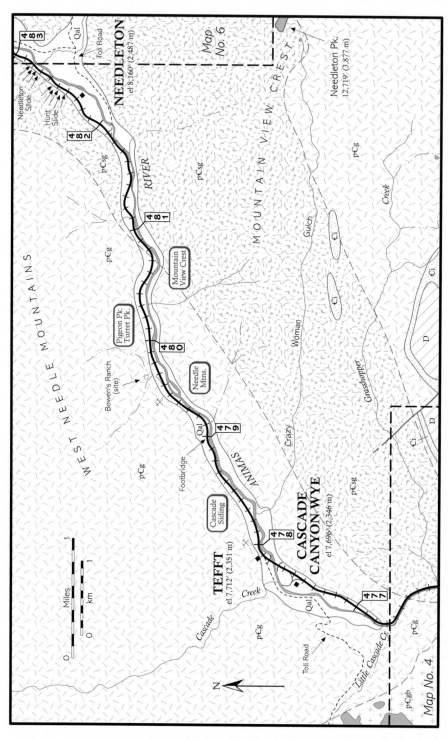

Map No. 5

44

478   SILVER STAR MINE.

Some lead, zinc, and silver were produced from this mine on the west side of the track. Four claims were staked along here in 1910 by Frederick Schaaf. These claims were leased by Oscar J. Grace of Oklahoma City in 1941, and a short time later they were taken over by Oscar Schaaf, who subsequently passed the claims on to his nephew, Ernie Schaaf. The Silver Star is the only remaining claim which still is owned by Ernie Schaaf.

Mile
478.4   CASCADE SIDING SIGN.
Elev. 7,785 ft (2,373 m)

At one time a siding, stock pen, section house, bunkhouse, and coal house were on the west side of the track. The railroad was completed to this point on June 7, 1882.

Milepost
479   VALLEY NARROWS.

A footbridge crosses the Animas. It is used by U.S. Forest Service personnel, fishermen and backpackers. The cabin across the river belongs to Ross McCausland, who built and operated the Ah! Wilderness Guest Ranch.

Mile
479.5   BITTER ROOT MINE.

The remains of this mining venture are on the west side of the track. Oscar Schaaf and his wife came to the Animas Canyon in the 1930s and took over some placer claims that had been staked by a man named Brown. The mine was named by Oscar's wife for her former home in the Bitterroot Mountains of Montana.

Mile
479.6   NEEDLE MOUNTAINS SIGN.

Throughout this section of the canyon are dramatic vistas of the sharp, jagged peaks to the northeast. Pigeon Peak, elevation 13,961 ft (4,255 m), is on the left; Turret Peak, elevation 13,619 ft (4,151 m) is on the right.

Trees are mostly tall aspens, some subalpine firs, willows, spruce, ponderosa pines, limber pines, lodgepole pines, and fewer Douglas firs.

479.7   SITE OF BOWEN'S RANCH.

In 1878, William C. Bowen and his wife, Jane, moved from Silverton and established a small ranch and way station for travelers on the toll road. The circumstances under which the couple left Silverton are clouded, but the Bowens had owned a grocery store and the Westminster Hall (saloon and bordello). Jane was known as "Aunt Jane" or "Sage Hen" while running her business in Silverton. The D&RG purchased a right-of-way through the Bowen property in 1880 and the Bowens returned to Silverton.

Oscar Schaaf built a small mill and concentrating table to process the small amount of ore he found in his claims. He moved two buildings from Cascade Siding to this site. Schaaf was the official fire warden for many years, and was well known for his mechanical abilities—including a motorized track car he built, the remains of which are still at Tefft. He deeded his property to another nephew, railroad conductor Mel Schaaf, who died in the early 1980s.

480.1   PIGEON PEAK—TURRET PEAK SIGN.

There are many chances for excellent photos of these peaks and of your train as it winds through the 20° curves along the Animas River.

480.5   MOUNTAIN VIEW CREST SIGN.

To the southeast, it is easy to see how this range acted as a barrier to the ice moving down the Animas canyon (p. 16). Glacially rounded gravel and boulders are strewn along the river. A waterfall is across the river.

A long-abandoned mine called the "Pajarito" (Little Parrot) was west of the track.

480.7   CONTACT OF GRANITE AND METAMORPHIC ROCKS.

Light gray Twilight Granite (p€g) was emplaced about 1.5 billion years ago. The banded, angular, blocky outcrops of older metamorphic gneiss and schist (p€sg) are markedly different from the rounded, smoothed, and glacially polished granite. Note the large size of the aspen trees.

481.5   LOWER END OF NEEDLETON PARK.

Upstream is an excellent view of Pigeon Peak. Portions of the San Juan Mountains, including the Needle Mountains, were designated as the San Juan Wilderness in 1965. In 1975, the area was enlarged to become the Weminuche Wilderness, the largest in the contiguous 48 states. It encompasses some 460,000 acres and extends eastward along the Continental Divide to Wolf Creek Pass. Four peaks, Mount Eolus, North Eolus, Sunlight Peak, and Windom Peak, are over 14,000 ft (4,270 m) and are popular destinations for mountain climbers (photo, p. 52).

482.31   ORIGINAL SITE OF NEEDLETON.
Elev. 8,160 ft (2,487 m)
The original Needleton station was washed away in the 1927 flood.

This was a stop on the stage road and the departure point for optimistic prospectors who flocked to Chicago Basin in the Needle Mountains in the 1880s. Interest in the area increased after the D&RG track reached Needleton June 14, 1882. Remarkably, a post office was established in May 1882 and lasted until January 10, 1919. The first postmaster was Theodore Schock, who had a post office at the top of Cascade Hill along the toll road but moved to Needleton when the Silverton Branch was completed. Additional history of the area is on pp. 76-77.

Mile
482.5   HUNT SLIDE.
This snow slide, named for early-day D&RG official A.C. Hunt, is also subject to mudslides. In January 1997 mud and debris from this slide were removed and the track was realigned to reduce the curvature.

Mile
482.8   NEEDLETON SNOWSLIDE.
This slide also comes down the steep western slope and often covers the track. From here to Silverton are numerous steep, almost vertical channel-like gullies that are pathways for huge snowslides (avalanches) that roar down the slopes after winter storms. Vegetation is unable to grow to any height in these paths. Trees, shrubs, rocks, and snow all end up on the track or in the river as huge mounds, as much as 40 to 80 ft deep. These snowslides are the primary reason the railroad is closed north of the Cascade Canyon Wye from November through May.

Mile
482.85   NEEDLE CREEK CANYON SIGN.
This sign is just above the Needleton snowslide. Needle Creek joins the Animas River from the east, flowing across an alluvial fan. The trail to Chicago Basin follows Needle Creek.

Look eastward up Needle Creek to the incredibly beautiful, horn-shaped peaks of the Needle Mountains that stand 500-1,000 ft (150-300 m) above the glaciers that filled the valleys. It is easy to see why the San Juans are called the "Alps of America."

Milepost
483   MILEPOST AT EDGE OF OPEN MEADOW. MAP NO. 6, P. 48.
Many wildflowers, grasses, and ferns grow in this meadow. In the early summer, Rocky Mountain iris thrive in these moist open meadows. The flowers are a variegated violet-blue color, about 2-3 inches long and on stalks 1-2 ft tall. The rootstocks of this plant have a strong, disagreeable odor and contain the poison, irisin, a violent emetic and cathartic. Yarrow

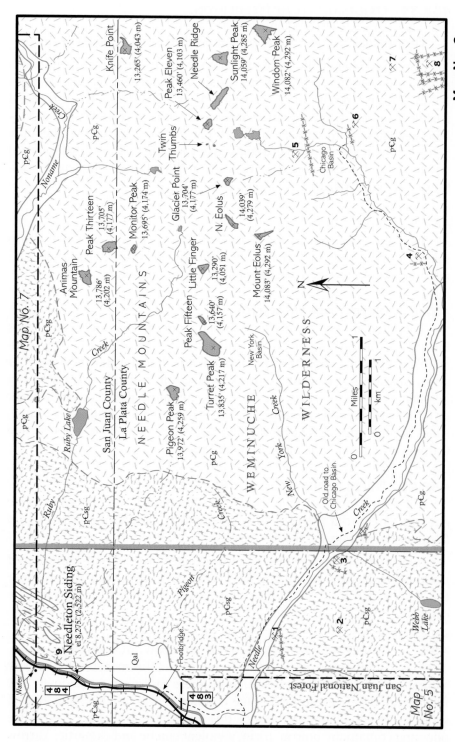

Knife Point
13,265' (4,043 m)

Peak Eleven
13,460' (4,103 m)

Needle Ridge

Sunlight Peak
14,059' (4,285 m)

Windom Peak
14,082' (4,292 m)

pCg

pCg

7

8

Noname Creek

Twin Thumbs

Peak Thirteen
13,705'
(4,177 m)

Monitor Peak
13,695' (4,174 m)

Glacier Point
13,704'
(4,177 m)

N. Eolus
14,039'
(4,279 m)

5

6

Chicago Basin

pCg

Animas Mountain
13,786'
(4,202 m)

Little Finger

Peak Fifteen
13,290'
(4,051 m)

Mount Eolus
14,083' (4,292 m)

N

4

San Juan County
La Plata County

N E E D L E   M O U N T A I N S

Peak Fifteen
13,640'
(4,157 m)

New York Basin

W I L D E R N E S S

Creek

pCsg

Ruby Lake

Pigeon Peak
13,972' (4,259 m)

Turret Peak
13,835' (4,217 m)

pCg

W E M I N U C H E

New York Creek

1
Miles
1
km
0

Old road to Chicago Basin

Ruby

pCsg

Creek

New Creek

Creek

pCg

Map No. 7

Map No. 5

Needleton Siding
el 8,275' (2,522 m)

Pigeon

pCsg

Footbridge

Needle Creek

3

2

pCg

pCg

Webb Lake

San Juan National Forest

Qal

9

Water

4 8 4

4 8 3

1

pCg

48

(milfoil or tansy) is another interesting flower that grows throughout the mountains from the lowest valleys to timberline. This flat-topped plant with many small white flowers in small heads or clusters grows to a height of 1 to 3 ft. The Indians used yarrow for a stimulant and tonic.

Mile
483.3   NEEDLETON FLAG STOP.
There is a footbridge here and trains stop to let off hikers, backpackers, and rafters going down the river. Most backpackers head for Chicago Basin and the high peaks of the Needle Mountains in the Weminuche Wilderness. Buildings across the river are privately owned. On the southern skyline is a good view of Mountain View Crest.

Mile
483.7   LA PLATA-SAN JUAN COUNTY LINE.
A sharp curve here is known as Dieckman's Curve, in honor of John Dieckman, D&RGW engineer who ran engine 473 into the river at this point because of a kink in the track caused by heat expansion (photo, p. 131).

Milepost
484   NEEDLETON SIDING SIGN.
Elev. 8,293 ft (2,528 m)
This 525-ft siding was placed here after the 1927 flood, when the river moved into a new channel between mile 481.8 and milepost 483. Aspens, birches, river willows, and subalpine firs, in addition to raspberries and countless wildflowers, thrive in this park.

Mile
484.2   SALLIE BOWMAN MINE.
This lode claim was located on March 30, 1883 by three miners. It changed hands several times before October 1897 at which time the property was purchased by Jerome E. Morse who patented the claim on December 31, 1898. He sold to the Treasury Consolidated Mining and Milling Co. who owned the property until 1949 when the county took over ownership. On January 2, 1958 Frank J. Adler acquired the prospect which has traces of gold in quartz-bearing pyrite veins. At the entrance to the mine was a boarding house, tool house, and blacksmith shop. There are no records of any ore ever being shipped from this mine.

Names of old mines shown on Map No. 6:	
1. Mastodon Mine	6. Little Jim Mine
2. Waterfall Mine	7. Black Giant Mine
3. List Mine	8. Jennie Hays Mine
4. Sheridan Mine	9. Sallie Bowman
5. Mt. Eolus Mine	

Newly-restored engine 497 steams past the Needleton water tank in July 1984.
(Kenneth T. Gustafson)

Northbound freight taking water at Needleton tank, mile 484.4, probably during the 1940s.
(Colorado Historical Society)

484.4   NEEDLETON TANK.

It takes lots of water to make the steam which propels your train up the 2.5% grade, so water tanks must be placed at strategic locations to quench the engine's thirst. A stop for water is made on both the up and down trips. The wooden water tank was retired in the 1960s, and a tank car body, located about 200 ft north of the old tank, now serves the same purpose. Water is piped from a small reservoir on the hill. The Needleton tank and the tank at Hermosa are the last wooden tanks on the Silverton Branch.

Traces of the old toll road are visible through the trees on the west slope. To the east is a good view of Pigeon Peak.

The west side of the Animas Canyon forms the base of the Twilight Peaks that are two miles to the west and stand one mile above the bottom of the canyon. These peaks are not visible from the train.

Mile

484.6   RUBY CREEK SIGN. MAP NO. 7, P. 54.

This creek plunges into the Animas River from the east. Several avalanche tracks and rock glaciers are along the west side of the track.

Trees include the ever-present willows and aspens. Alpine fir, Englemann spruce, and limber pine are common at this elevation.

A Durango-bound D&SNG train, powered by engine 478, winds along the tumbling Animas River between Tall Timber and Tank Creek.
         (Kenneth T. Gustafson)

Geologist Whitman Cross took this spectacular photo July 12, 1901, from the summit of Mountain View Crest looking northward across Needle Creek Canyon to the beautiful faceted horns of Pigeon Peak, Turret Peak, and Mt. Eolus, from left to right.

(U.S. Geological Survey)

This magnificent view of Electric, Arrow, and Vestal Peaks, from right to left, was taken in August 1903 by geologist Ernest Howe. He was standing across Elk Creek on a high ridge looking south-southwest. *(U.S. Geological Survey)*

485   GRANITE CLIFFS.

For the next four miles the track is built on Precambrian Twilight Granite, named for the Twilight peaks in the West Needle Mountains. Notice how the light gray granite cliffs on both sides of the track have been rounded, smoothed, and polished by the Animas glacier.

Mile
485.4   NO NAME SNOWSLIDE.

This snowslide descends the steep western valley opposite the point where Noname Creek cascades across a moraine to join the Animas River.

A short distance north of this slide, at mile 485.5, are Noname Rapids which present a real challenge for rafters and kayakers who make their way down the river from May until mid-July. Watch for large, smooth rocks in the river at this narrow bottleneck.

Mile
485.7   MOUNTAIN VIEW CREST SIGN.

There is a good view to the south of this range. When the water level is low, potholes in the river channel are visible.

Milepost
486   HIGH PEAKS OF THE GRENADIER RANGE.

Glimpses of these beautiful peaks are visible to the northeast. Granite outcrops have been rounded and polished by the Animas Glacier moving slowly southward.

Mile
486.5   SITE OF MUDSLIDES.

During **Railfest 1999** heavy rains washed out the track at this troublesome location. On August 17, 1999, the first southbound train passed the washout, but the two later trains were forced to return to Silverton. During the two full days required to repair the damage, two trains ran daily between Durango and Cascade Wye, while the *Eureka* and Galloping Goose No. 5 continued their scheduled runs between Rockwood and Cascade.

Milepost
487   STEEPEST GRADE ON SILVERTON BRANCH.

Even though the track profile states the ruling grade is a constant 2.5%, for the next mile the actual grade is 3% with short sections of nearly 4%. Now the fireman is shoveling coal at a furious pace to keep steam up.

Mile
487.15   TENMILE CREEK TUMBLES INTO THE ANIMAS.
Elev. 8,641 ft (2,634 m)

It is believed that the toll road builders named this stream that is exactly 10 miles from Silverton. In 1880, Franz Armine Schneider and his family moved to this open level area along Tenmile Creek and started an establishment known as Ten Mile House. Horses could be changed, and as

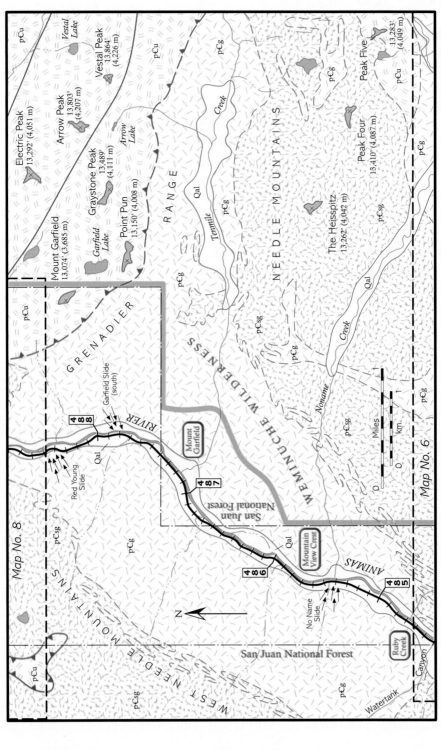

pCu

Vestal Lake

Vestal Peak
13,864'
(4,226 m)

Electric Peak
13,292' (4,051 m)

Arrow Peak
13,803'
(4,207 m)

pCu

pCg

Mount Garfield
13,074' (3,685 m)

Graystone Peak
13,489'
(4,111 m)

Garfield Lake

Point Pun
13,150' (4,008 m)

Arrow Lake

pCg

pCu

Creek

pCg

pCg

R A N G E

Qal

Tenmile

pCg

pCu

G R E N A D I E R

Peak Five
13,283'
(4,049 m)

pCu

Peak Four
13,410' (4,087 m)

N E E D L E   M O U N T A I N S

The Heisspitz
13,262' (4,042 m)

pCg

pCsg

Qal

pCg

Garfield Slide
(south)

RIVER

Qal

Red Young Slide

488

Mount
Garfield

W E M I N U C H E   W I L D E R N E S S

San Juan National Forest

487

Noname

pCsg

pCg

Creek

pCsg

pCg

0   1
Miles

0   1
km.

Map No. 6

pCg

Map No. 8

pCsg

pCg

N

Qal

Mountain
View Crest

486

A N I M A S

485

No Name
Slide

pCu

pCsg

W E S T   N E E D L E   M O U N T A I N S

pCg

San Juan National Forest

Ruby
Creek

Canyon

Watertank

pCg

Rocky mountain splendor in the Animas canyon. This lovely view, just south of milepost 486, looks northeast toward Mount Garfield in the Grenadier Range. The columbines growing beside the track are Colorado s state flower. (Richard L. Hunter)

Allen Nossaman so aptly described conditions of travel on the toll road, Tenmile Creek was "frequently the transition point from moderate to miserable weather for northbound travel during the winter in the canyon." The old toll road still is visible in the trees above the track. Schneider kept a team of dogs which often were called upon to carry mail, supplies, and even drinking water to Silverton on sleds when the track was blocked.

Mile
487.25 MOUNT GARFIELD SIGN.

This peak is visible on the westbound trip.

Mile
487.9 GARFIELD SNOWSLIDE.

Most winters this slide crosses the river and plows into the track. Two large slides come down the steep slopes of Mount Garfield; the northern slide is at mile 489.5. From here to milepost 495, the train crosses the paths of many snowslides, making this the most difficult section of track to open. Because so much debris is carried in the snow, rotary plows could never be used. Every spring, locomotives equipped with pilot plows pull flatcars loaded with bulldozers to this area. The bulldozers then go to work clearing the track (photo, p. 111).

During the 1980s, the D&SNG realigned the track through this section to reduce the curves and ease the hard pull for longer trains. Listen how the sound of the locomotive's exhaust changes as grade eases from here to milepost 494.

The southern snowslide off Mount Garfield at mile 487.8, as it looked June 4, 1965.

(F. W. Osterwald)

488   PLACER MINING OPERATION.

Remnants of a placer mining operation are across the river. The operation was not successful because the sand, rocks, and boulders of many sizes are mixed together in a jumbled manner, making it difficult to separate and find flakes of gold.

Mile
488.5   RED YOUNG SLIDE.

This slide, on the west side of the track, was named for an early-day engineer, William (Red) Young, who was killed when his engine slammed into a snowslide in 1897. This was one of the few railroad fatalities that resulted from a snowslide. Sometimes, when the slides were particularly deep, it was easier to tunnel through than to remove all the snow from the track. Additional details on snow problems are on pp. 105-108.

Milepost
489   UNNAMED STREAM JOINS ANIMAS. MAP NO. 8, P. 58.

This steep mountain stream on the west has its source on the southern slope of Snowden Peak, named in honor of Francis M. Snowden, a miner who built the first cabin in Silverton in 1874.

In this area, the Animas Canyon is about 4,200 ft deep, and a little less than three miles wide.

The boundary between Precambrian granite and Precambrian metamorphic rocks is very irregular and indistinct. The layered outcrops of gneiss and schist stand vertical in blocky cliffs. Granite outcrops are smoother and more rounded.

Mile
489.5   CROSS MAJOR FAULT ZONE.

Map No. 8 (p. 58) shows a major thrust fault that crosses the Animas Valley at this point. Precambrian Uncompahgre Quartzite (pCu) is faulted against Precambrian gneisses and schists (pCsg). Note the tight folds in the shiny, gray quartzite which was deposited as sand by rivers flowing into a sea about 1 billion years ago. Between here and milepost 492 are several more east-west trending faults.

The northern Garfield Slide comes down the north slope of the peak through a narrow, V-shaped fault valley. Snow may remain piled in the stream until mid-June.

Mile
489.85   CROSS ANIMAS RIVER.

This two-span, 222-ft steel deck plate girder bridge was installed in 1964. The track makes a wide curve here before entering the main part of Elk Park. The best view of the old four-span through truss timber bridge built in 1884 is visible to the west while crossing the "new" bridge. The old

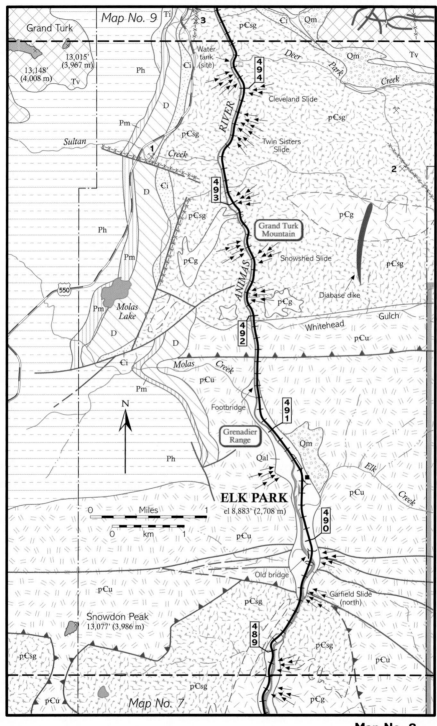

Grand Turk

13,148'
(4,008 m)

13,015'
(3,967 m)

Tv

Ti

3

p€sg

€i

Qm

Water
tank
(site)

494

€i

Ph

D

Deer

Qm

Tv

Park

Creek

Cleveland Slide

Pm

p€sg

p€sg

Sultan

Creek

1

RIVER

Twin Sisters
Slide

2

D

€i

493

p€sg

Grand Turk
Mountain

p€g

Ph

Pm

p€g

ANIMAS

Snowshed Slide

p€sg

550

Pm

Molas
Lake

Diabase dike

Whitehead

Gulch

D

492

p€u

D

€i

Molas

Creek

Pm

p€u

N

Footbridge

491

Grenadier
Range

Qm

Ph

Qal

Elk

ELK PARK
el 8,883' (2,708 m)

p€u

Creek

0   Miles   1

490

0   km   1

p€u

Old bridge

p€u

Garfield Slide
(north)

Snowdon Peak
13,077' (3,986 m)

p€sg

p€sg

489

p€sg

p€sg

p€u

p€u

p€sg

p€g

p€u

Map No. 8

58

bridge was abandoned in 1964 because the abutments became weakened during spring runoffs.

490.15 MINCO SPUR.

A two-car spur has been used occasionally by a small uranium mining operation uphill to the west.

490.3 CROSS ELK CREEK.

To the west, across the river, folds in the metamorphic Uncompahgre Quartzite (pЄu) are clearly visible.

490.5 ELK PARK.
Elev. 8,883 ft (2,707 m)

A siding and wye are located at this site. At one time there was also a section house, bunkhouse and a coal bin. This station is also a flag stop for fishermen and for backpackers who use the steep trail along Elk Creek into the Needle Mountains. The Colorado Trail follows Elk Creek eastward.

The famous Colorado Trail covers 489 miles through Colorado's remote high country along the Continental Divide from the mountains southwest of Denver to Durango. Westbound hikers descend into Elk Park, cross the Animas River on a footbridge at MP 491.3, and climb the steep slope along Molas Creek into the West Needle Mountains.

The frantic pace of laying hand-hewn ties on the roadbed and spiking down 30-lb steel rail continued without interruption throughout the spring of 1882, and by June 27, 1882, construction trains were running to Elk Park. In 1884, a wye was built so trains could be turned when the track between Silverton and Elk Park was blocked by snowslides. A stub turnout with a harp-type switch stand joined the two legs of the wye. This unusual switch stand, the last one used in Colorado, was gone by 1973. At one time there were stock pens for loading and unloading sheep.

This open, grassy park is filled with wildflowers. In the spring, white candytuft is common, along with dandelions. Dandelions, which are socially unacceptable in city lawns, are beautiful in the mountains in early June. The flowers and leaves are a favorite food of grouse, elk, deer, bear, and porcupine. The roots have been used for centuries for tonics, diuretics, and mild laxatives. The leaves are used in salads and the blossoms for making wine. Summer brings the columbines, mountain parsley, ferns, Indian paintbrushes, shrub cinquefoil, penstemons, lupines, primroses, and gentians. In September, yarrow, goldenrod, fall asters, and daisies are abundant.

Some avalanche tracks are directly across the river. A large moraine (Qm on Map No. 8, p. 58) is along the east side of the valley. The river has reworked the morainal deposits and combined them with stream gravel.

On August 11, 1903, Ernest Howe captured this afternoon scene looking south along the Animas River about a mile above Elk Park. Mount Garfield dominates the skyline, while Electric Peak is on the far left, and Graystone Peak is in between. These peaks are part of the Grenadier Range.

(U.S. Geological Survey)

491.2 GRENADIER RANGE SIGN.

This sign is visible on the return trip. Look southward down the valley for glimpses of Graystone and Electric Peaks, along with a very good view of Mount Garfield. To the south, momentary glimpses of Arrow and Vestal Peaks may be seen before the train leaves Elk Park. Map No. 7 (p. 54) shows the location of these high peaks of the Grenadier Range that stood above the surrounding ice fields.

491.3 MOLAS CREEK.

This stream, which heads on Molas Pass, joins the Animas here. A footbridge across the Animas River.

The rocks in the river channel are stained a reddish-brown due to chemicals in the water which have been leached from the mill tailing ponds that operated near Silverton at one time (photo, p. 63).

491.65 TRACK CROSSES LARGE EAST-WEST THRUST FAULT.

491.95 WHITEHEAD GULCH.
Elev. 8,981 ft (2,737 m)

Sometime after the Silverton water tank at mile 494.2 was removed in 1924 (photo, p. 63), a water spout was rigged at the mouth of this steep gulch and was used for locomotive water into the 1960s. The spout and flume were washed away sometime between then and the 1970 flood.

Between Whitehead Gulch and the Snowshed Slide at mile 492.5 is the final stretch of steep grade before reaching Silverton.

The old toll road is visible on the hillside to the west, across the river. Old rails lying in the Animas are stark reminders of past floods.

Whitehead Gulch follows an east-west fault that is easily seen looking west across the river. The fault brings the Uncompahgre Quartzite in contact with gneiss and schist. There are also two small, irregular masses of reddish-pink granite that crop out on each side of the river. This gulch is near the southern margin of the highly mineralized area along the southern flank of the Silverton caldera.

492.5 SNOWSHED SLIDE.

The timber side sills and concrete walls are all that remain of a 339-ft long snow shed built in 1890 to protect the track from two slides that converged at this point. The shed was burned July 23, 1917, and was replaced by a 400-ft shed. The date this second shed was removed is not known. At one time there was a small shack where a caretaker lived during the snowshed days. The building was destroyed during a fire in 1981.

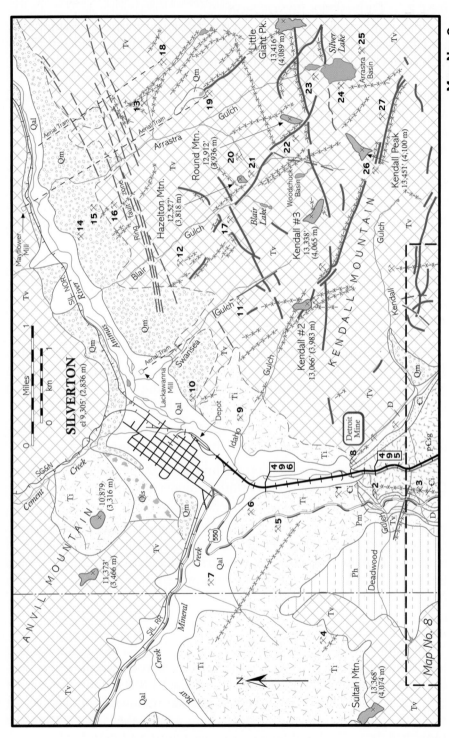

SILVERTON
el 9,305' (2,836 m)

ANVIL MOUNTAIN

11,373'
(3,466 m)

10,879'
(3,316 m)

Cement Creek

Mayflower Mill

Aerial Tram

Lackawanna Mill

Depot

Arrastra

Blair Gulch

Swansea Gulch

Hazelton Mtn.
12,527'
(3,818 m)

Round Mtn.
12,912'
(3,936 m)

Blair Lake

Kendall #3
13,338'
(4,065 m)

Kendall #2
13,066' (3,983 m)

KENDALL MOUNTAIN

Little Giant Pk.
13,416'
(4,089 m)

Silver Lake

Arrastra Basin

Kendall Peak
13,451' (4,100 m)

Kendall Gulch

Woodchuck Basin

Detroit Mine

Deadwood Gulch

Sultan Mtn.
13,368'
(4,074 m)

Mineral Creek

Bear Creek

Arrastra Gulch

Ring Fault zone

Idaho

N

Miles

km

Map No. 8

View northward below milepost 495. This dramatic photo, taken in the fall when the water level is low, reveals how iron-rich minerals from mine dumps and mine drainages have been carried into the Animas River and deposited on the rocks as rusty, yellow-brown iron oxide stains. (Anthony Frank)

Names of old mines shown on Map No. 9:
1. Champion Mine
2. Detroit Mine
3. King Mine
4. Belcher (Sultan Mtn.)
5. Montezuma Mine
6. Empire Tunnel
7. North Star (Sultan Mtn.)
8. Marcella Mine
9. Idaho Mine
10. Mighty Monarch
11. Scranton City Mine
12. Blair Mountain Mine
13. Little Giant Mine
14. Amy Tunnel
15. Legal Tender Tunnel
16. Aspen Group
17. Happy Jack
18. Black Prince Mine
19. Shenandoah-Dives Mine
20. Unity Mine
21. Nevada Mine
22. New York Mine
23. Silver Lake Mine
24. Iowa Mine
25. Royal Tiger Mine
26. Titusville Mine
27. Buckeye Mine

Following the removal of the water tank that once stood at mile 494.2, D&RGW officials took this photo in May 1924 showing the wooden platform remaining at the site. (Album of Water Rights, Center for Southwest Studies,

Ft. Lewis College)

From here to milepost 495 is an area with many small snowslides that usually do not cause major problems for the railroad.

Mile
492.8   GRAND TURK MOUNTAIN SIGN.
Views of the majestic twin summits are visible to the northwest.

Mile
493.35   MOLAS MINE ON THE WEST.
Look up the steep valley of Sultan Creek for a glimpse of the Molas Mine, located about 1,200 ft above the Animas River. It produced ore from a mineralized fault.

From here to Silverton, hundreds of dangerous mine dumps, the remains of shacks, and collapsing mine buildings are visible on the steep hillsides offering stark evidence of Silverton's rich mining heritage. Maps 8 and 9 show the locations of many mines in the area and illustrate the complicated geology.

Mile
493.6   TWIN SISTERS SLIDE.

Milepost
494   CLEVELAND SLIDE.
Both slides run regularly each year.

Mile
494.2   SITE OF WATER TANK.
The Silverton water tank was located on the east side of the track, a short distance south of the Deer Park Creek. The tank was removed in 1924 (photo, p. 63). The cement foundations still are visible along the east side of the track.

Mile
494.6   REMAINS OF ORE TIPPLE ON EAST.
The remains of an old boiler are also at this site. Across the river, the bucket cable from the King Mine is visible.

Just beyond the ore tipple, the track crosses Kendall Creek which heads on Kendall Mountain, named for James W. Kendall, one of the original owners of the famous North Star mine.

Mile
494.65   KING MINE.
Remains of this mine (mine 3 on Map No. 9, p. 62) are on the hillside across the river in a steep gulch aptly named Cataract. An aerial tram brought silver and copper ore to a loading dock and spur track located at mile 494.8.

495   DEADWOOD GULCH. MAP NO. 9, P. 62.

Across the river and high on the steep slope of this gulch was the Detroit Mine (mine 2). It produced silver, zinc, and copper. The creek flows under the remains of the old mine building. A spur track to the tram station along the main track was removed in 1924.

495.25 CROSS ANIMAS RIVER.

This is the last crossing of the Animas before arriving in Silverton. The bridge is a deck timber structure that has been featured in countless railroad photographs.

Just beyond the bridge, the remains of the Champion Mine (mine 1) can be seen on the west side of the track. Copper sulfide and silver-bearing ores, along with some zinc, were produced from the mine in considerable quantities. A spur track to the ore bin was removed in 1924. The mine is located on the contact of a Tertiary quartz monzonite (Ti) mass that was intruded (emplaced) as a fluid into the Ouray and Leadville Limestones about 10 million years ago. Quartz monzonite is a light tan-to-buff-to-brown colored, fine-grained igneous rock. Other workings up the hill near the highway on this same contact account for the bright green copper-bearing minerals that are being deposited along the steep gulch from water that flows out of the mine portal.

496.15 CROSS MINERAL CREEK.

This 112-ft steel plate through-girder bridge was built in 1907 for the standard gauge Colorado Springs & Cripple Creek District RR and installed here in 1916.

On the west, just above the valley floor, are remnants of the Hercules Mine and Melville Mill. A spur track to the mill joined the mainline at milepost 496.

496.3   SILVERTON WYE.

While you are visiting Silverton, your train will back down to this wye, where it will turn around and be brought back up to 12th and Blair Streets for re-boarding.

Silverton has the distinction of being the only town in the United States once served by four narrow gauge railroads. In addition to the former D&RG on which you are riding, the Silverton Railroad, the Silverton, Gladstone and Northerly Railroad, and the Silverton Northern Railroad traversed the alpine canyons to serve the mines to the north and northwest of Silverton (Map No. 9, p. 62). Additional data concerning these railroads are on p. 80.

496.7 SILVERTON DEPOT.

In 1969, the D&RGW donated the depot to the San Juan Historical Society. The D&SNG purchased the building in 1985. An agent is on duty in the summer months. In 1999 a new freight yard museum opened at the depot. The historic buildings around the depot are identified, and displays show freight cars, minerals, and mining equipment from the area. Also, descriptions of the three narrow gauge shortlines that went from Silverton to several nearby mining districts are shown (pp. 65, 80). The entrance fee to the museum is included in your train ticket fare. K-37 No. 493 is on display behind the depot.

496.9 SILVERTON.
Elev. 9,305 ft (2,836 m)

Welcome to Silverton. First known as Baker's Park, the name of the new camp along the now placid, slow-moving Animas River was soon changed. As one early miner put it so succinctly: "We may not have any gold, but we have silver by the ton!" Details of Silverton's history are on pp. 77-81.

You will have time to enjoy lunch, visit the shops and historic sites in town before four long—and loud—blasts of the engine whistle summon everyone back to their coach for the return trip to Durango. Try to visit the newly restored Town Hall that was almost completely destroyed by fire November 30, 1992.

In 1949, the movie, "Ticket to Tomahawk" was filmed on the Silverton Branch and in Silverton. The depot was renamed "Epitaph," and RGS engine 20 (now at the Colorado Railroad Museum at Golden) became engine 1, the Emma Sweeney.

(Collection of Edna Sanborn)

SUGGESTIONS FOR YOUR RETURN TRIP:

If you plan to follow the Mile by Mile Guide on the return trip to Durango, note that the mileposts are on the *left* side of the train. The mileposts obviously will be in reverse order. Perhaps there were particular locations you missed on the morning trip, so plan ahead for points of interest that you may want to photograph and enjoy.

As the train passes the depot, Sultan Mountain, elevation 13,361 ft (4,072 m), is to the southwest, and the twin summits of Grand Turk, both over 13,000 ft elevation (3,960 m), are on the left of Sultan Mountain. Directly north of Silverton is Anvil Mountain. Kendall Mountain, on the eastern skyline, was the site of many rich mines. As of 1995, no mines are operating in the Silverton District. Map No. 9, p. 62, shows a generalized geologic map of the district and the location of some nearby mines. Most mineral deposits were formed within the last 10 million years.

After your train passes the wye and turns south toward the Animas Canyon, a dramatic view of Mount Garfield in the distance is a prelude of more spectacular scenery to enjoy on the return trip.

On May 2, 1992, newly-restored engine 482 pulled the first train of the season to Silverton, proudly flying the Colorado state flag and the Stars and Stripes as it passed the Silverton depot. In 1999 the depot and yards were converted into a museum. (D.B. Osterwald)

HISTORY

DURANGO

Durango's birth was the direct result of the Denver and Rio Grande Railway's decision to build its expanding railroad system into the silver-ribbed San Juan Mountains. Colorado's mining camps got their start when mineral deposits were discovered, but no real growth was achieved until the railroads, most of them "slim-gauge," arrived to take the ore to market and to bring supplies and people to the mines. As early as 1878, D&RG locating engineers started surveying possible routes into the mining districts of the San Juans. An article in *The La Plata Miner*, published in Silverton, April 5, 1879, stated:

> The struggle for priority of railway possession of the San Juan has now actively begun, and the shrill whistle of the locomotive and rumbling of cars over rocky beds will soon be echoing from the sides of these mountains." By October 25, 1879 another article in *The La Plata Miner* reported: "A D&RG surveying party is now working on locating the line for the railroad in Animas Canyon. Surveyors have to be let down with ropes over the walls of the canyon in order to get the level.

In December 1879, the D&RG purchased the Animas Canyon Toll Road which was built in 1876 to connect Silverton with Animas City. The railroad laid track on portions of the toll road between Animas City and Rockwood, and between Cascade Canyon wye and Silverton. But the D&RG surveyors decided to blast out a roadbed in the narrow canyon high above the Animas River (the Highline) instead of following the steep toll road northward from Rockwood.

The Animas River has been called Rio Animas (River of Souls), Rio de las Animas, Rio las Animas, Las Animas, and Rio de las Animas de Perdidas (River of Lost Souls) in the literature and on old maps. The correct name is Animas River.

About 100 years before the D&RG started surveying and building its line to Silverton, the southern flank of the San Juan Mountains had been explored by the Spanish. In 1761 and 1775 Juan Maria Rivera led expeditions into what is now southwestern Colorado searching for gold and silver. In August 1776 Silvestre Escalante came from New Mexico seeking a route from Santa Fe to the California missions.

The next group of prospectors arrived in 1860, led by Captain Charles Baker who came to the San Juans via the Lake Fork of the Gunnison and its headwaters at Cinnamon Pass. From there, they descended to the open park on the upper Animas, panning for gold along the way. By fall, the men followed the Animas River southward and made a quick trip to New Mexico for supplies. They returned to Colorado in mid-October and spent the winter at a site known later as Elbert, Baker's Bridge, the First Animas City, or Animas City No. 1. The six men continued prospecting during 1861, staking claims in Arrastra, Cunningham, and Eureka Gulches, but left the mountains after the Civil War started, having found very little placer gold.

The San Juans were not invaded again until after the Civil War, when many penniless and battle-weary veterans headed west in search of a new life; prospecting seemed a possible way to make a quick fortune. Inevitably, clashes between the Utes and the prospectors and settlers increased, and the interlopers demanded that "the Utes must go." However the government made little effort to keep intruders from entering the Indian lands. In 1863, the Tabeguache Utes signed the vague, ill-defined Conejos Treaty with the government, which only increased the tension between the newcomers and the Indians.

Neither side lived up to this treaty, and in 1868 a new agreement was signed which further restricted the size of the Indian lands and brought an uneasy truce between the whites and the Utes. With each treaty, the Utes lost more of their land in return for annual allotments of food, clothing, and supplies. The 1868 treaty had barely gone into effect when promising reports of gold in the San Juans brought even more prospectors onto Indian lands. Finally, on May 21, 1873, the Indians signed the Brunot Treaty with the U.S. and 3.5 million acres of land were opened for legal entry by miners and settlers. At that time the Utes still had over 15 million acres of land in Colorado Territory. After signing, the Utes lost their sacred San Juan Mountains in return for a guaranteed reservation and annual subsidies. Present-day Indian reservations are along the Utah–Colorado–New Mexico boundaries.

The last real Indian scare in the Animas Valley occurred after the Meeker Massacre in northwestern Colorado, September 29, 1879. Fort Lewis, a military fort, established in or near Pagosa Springs in 1872. To protect settlers from a possible Indian uprising after the Meeker Massacre, about 600 troops from Fort Lewis, under the command of Gen. Edward Hatch, marched to Animas City where a sod fort, called Fort Flagler, was built. There were no skirmishes with the Indians, but the troops remained in the area until January 1880.

La Plata County was created out of the western half of Conejos County which was laid out by the 1874 Colorado Territorial Legislature with the county seat in Silverton. Two years later, La Plata was divided into San Juan County with the new county seat again at Silverton. The southern half retained the name, La Plata County, and the county seat was now in Parrott City, a struggling placer mining camp along the La Plata River west of Durango.

Animas City, the first community in the lower Animas Valley, grew around a number of struggling farms and small ranches. By 1876, the settlement had about 30 cabins, a school, saloons, and supply companies for miners heading to the high county. A flour mill was built in 1877, postal service started May 24, 1877, and the town was incorporated December 24, 1878.

Durango, on the other hand, was a "company" town owned and laid out two miles south of Animas City by the D&RG Railway in the spring of 1880. This was the result of Animas City declining the railroad's offer to donate land and invest in the line. With the completion of the Silverton Branch, Animas City merchants began relocating to the new town (see also pp. 13, 14), and in 1881 the La Plata county government followed suit.

Perhaps the Animas City newspaper's most famous quotation concerned the location of the new town of Durango, as proposed by the D&RG. The editor quipped on May 1, 1880: "The Bank of San Juan has issued a circular in which it is stated that a branch office will be opened at the 'new town of Durango on the Rio Animas.' Where the new town of Durango is to be, or not to be, God and the D&RG Railroad only know. If they are in cahoots we ask for special dispensation." The D&RG ignored Animas City and laid out a company town two miles below Animas City. But it was not until October 28, 1947 that Animas City formally was annexed to Durango.

Rio Grande officials borrowed the name "Durango" from a city in central Mexico, obviously still thinking of their original plans to connect Denver with Mexico City. It is difficult to comprehend today how Durango, to which all supplies came great distances by pack trains, could be laid out in the spring of 1880 so that by September lots were selling for $250 to $500, a brickyard and lumber yard had been built, and a smelter was under construction. *The La Plata Miner* reported December 18, 1880, that many people were coming to Durango from Leadville. In fact, Durango's first newspaper press was brought by pack train from Leadville, and the paper first was published using a tent for an office. The owner, publisher, and editor was Mrs. C.W. Romney, a petite, good-looking widow who put out the first issue of *The Durango Record* December 29, 1880. On January 10, 1881, the newspaper moved into a "spacious" office and plant 22 × 50 ft in size.

Railroad construction continued at a rapid pace. By January 1881, the D&RG owned 3,000 freight cars, had purchased or contracted for 124 locomotives, had 684 miles of track, and the original iron rails had been replaced with steel rails on many routes. Durango was eagerly awaiting the arrival of the railroad, which was being extended from Antonito, Colorado, over Cumbres Pass, and crisscrossing the Colorado-New Mexico border before turning northwest toward Durango.

View west of Durango in 1881. D&RG track is barely visible in front of the buildings on the left. The graded area in the foreground is First St., now Main Ave.

(Center for Southwest Studies, Fort Lewis College)

Every week newspapers reported the number of miles the track was from Durango. On July 7, 1881, *The Durango Herald* duly announced: "The railway is now within 18 miles of Durango and well informed persons express confidence that the track layers will reach this city before the close of the present month." Construction continued at a breakneck pace in spite of trouble keeping enough men on the work gangs, delays in the arrival of ties and rails at the end of track, and accidents. One accident about 20 miles east of Durango injured two men when a blast was set off prematurely. Finally, the first construction train arrived in the "city" of Durango July 27, 1881, and the telegraph lines were completed July 30. The first passenger train steamed into town August 1, 1881. An interesting account of the arrival of that first train appears in Volume I of the *Pioneers of the San Juan County*:

> The track reached the corporate limits about 11 a.m. and when at 5 o'clock in the evening, the construction train reached G Street [now 9th Street] in about the center of the city, the enthusiasm could no longer be restrained. Men, women, and children lined Railroad Street [now Narrow Gauge Avenue] for nearly its whole length; sidewalks, doorways, and windows were crowded; the members of the City Band assembled at the corner of G and Railroad and commenced playing lively airs, and this of course brought out everybody.

> Soon the officers of the City government appeared on the scene, in a body, headed by the Mayor with a silver spike and a hammer in hand— when all were assembled, our worthy townsman, J.L. Pennington, stepped forward, and with a claw bar extracted the iron spike inserted

by the railroad men, then Mayor Taylor, spike mall in hand inserted a silver spike made from La Plata County ore, and with three terrific blows drove the spike clean in, there by uniting Durango by a steel band, with the civilized world.

The railroad and the city planned a gala celebration for August 5, 1881, but a special train of dignitaries from Denver did not arrive until the next day because of a severe washout east of town. The program proceeded, however, with a parade of the city police, city officials in carriages, and Fort Lewis sent two companies of infantry, an artillery squad, and their military band. Following the parade there were races, a ball game, a shooting match, and the day ended with a dance at the new smelter.

The first freight train brought carloads of railway supplies for the Silverton Branch and an elegant stagecoach to carry passengers to and from the depot and hotels. The Durango post office, which opened November 19, 1880, ranked third in the state according to the number of business transactions, yet the town was less than a year old.

Throughout the 1890s, as Durango's population fluctuated between 4,000 and 7,000 citizens, two smelters processed ores from the San Juan mines, coal mines opened, coke ovens were built along Lightner Creek west of town and served by the Rio Grande Southern, Durango's second railroad.

Across the Animas River, opposite the railroad yards, was the smelter built in 1881 by the San Juan and New York Mining and Smelting Co. The company started in Silverton, but moved to Durango to be closer to a coal

View east of Durango after the 1889 fire destroyed most of the buildings in the 1000 block of the business district. D&RG track is visible just behind the few buildings in the foreground that were not burned. (Animas Museum, Durango)

supply to process the gold, silver, lead, zinc, and copper ores. Between 1948 and 1963, the plant processed uranium and vanadium ores. During the late 1970s and early 1980s, all traces of the plant and tailings were removed in a massive clean up effort directed by the Environmental Protection Agency.

Electric lights and telephones were installed, and streetcars operated between the depot northward along Durango's Main Avenue from 1891 to 1920. The first automobile arrived in Durango on a railroad flatcar in 1902.

During the first half of the twentieth century, Durango maintained its position as the industrial, agricultural, and cultural center of southwestern Colorado. Serious efforts to attract tourists to the area started when the first automobile roads were built to Silverton and Mesa Verde. Chamber of Commerce brochures proclaimed the wonders of the San Juans, the "Switzerland of America." As highways were improved and expanded in the 1930s, the need for railroads in the San Juans diminished.

View southwest of Durango circa 1910. The smelter must have been working full-time, judging from the amount of smoke coming from the stacks. Durango s prosperity was due largely to the smelter and to the railroads. Population was about 9,000 at this time.

(Collection of Partridge Studio, Durango)

Durango became the center of rail activity in southwestern Colorado, with branches going south to Farmington, New Mexico (photos, pp. 98-99, 102), north to Silverton, eastward on the mainline to Alamosa via Cumbres Pass, and west to Rico, Telluride, and Ridgway on the Rio Grande Southern Railroad.

In 1890 the resolute Otto Mears, famous toll road and railroad builder of southwestern Colorado, decided to build a fourth railroad from Ridgeway to Durango that followed a convoluted 162 mile route via the booming mining camps of Telluride, Ophir, and Rico. The Rio Grande Southern was completed in 1892 and was profitable for only one year before the Silver Panic of 1893 forced the company into receivership. The RGS limped along until 1952 when this legendary railroad was abandoned and the tracks removed (photos, pp. 123, 136, 137).

After the Rio Grande Southern was abandoned, an exciting era of rail-roading in the San Juans was almost at an end. Starting in the mid-1950s, the D&RGW repeatedly petitioned the Interstate Commerce Commission (ICC) to abandon the Silverton Branch, but fortunately the request was denied. The railroad then accepted the fact that it was in the business of carrying tourists between Durango and Silverton on an unforgettable "Journey to Yesterday." Ridership increased each year, but the Rio Grande was anxious to get out of the tourist business. In 1981 the branch was purchased by Charles E. Bradshaw, Jr., who later sold the D&SNG to First American Railways, Inc. in 1997, and in 1998 the line was purchased by American Heritage Railways.

ROCKWOOD

Exactly when the beautiful, secluded mountain valley now known as Rockwood was first settled is lost in the mists of time. It is believed, however, that Levi Carson was the first to settle here, and for several years the site was called Carson's. The Rev. Joseph W. Pickett is credited with naming the small settlement. If it was named for Silverton residents William, James, or Thomas Rockwood, this fact also has been lost. But by July 8, 1878, Rockwood had a post office.

After the D&RG acquired the toll road, it was used to transport men and supplies to Rockwood which became the marshalling point for the construction through the Animas Canyon gorge and northward to Silverton.

D&RG grading crews started working north of Durango even before the first work train arrived in Durango on July 27, 1881. The grading and bridging to Rockwood was completed by September 30 and crews finished spiking rail onto newly laid ties on November 26, 1881. Passenger service between Durango and Rockwood did not begin until January 1882, however, because work trains were busy transporting laborers, ties, rails, spikes, black powder, and other equipment to Rockwood. No doubt laborers camped here while the shelf track high above the Animas River was under construction.

By 1882, a depot, section house, bunkhouse, and coal house were completed, and the growing community had a post office, school, general store, saloon, sawmill, cemetery, restaurant, dry goods store, barn, corral, a doctor, and a hotel. When the Rio Grande Southern Railroad reached Rico in 1891, the toll road from Rockwood to Rico was no longer needed, and Rockwood's importance soon faded.

The March 18, 1882, Silverton *La Plata Miner* reported:

> Misters Ford and Bennett arrived in Durango on Wednesday with 69 head of mules and a camp equipment for 50 men. Working force on the railroad between Silverton and Cascade is being daily increased. By April 1, the road will be opened 6 miles this side of Rockwood, thus eliminating the dangerous stage ride down Cascade Hill.

Before the RGS railroad was completed to Rico in 1891, the stage route to Rico began in Rockwood, shown in this interesting photograph. Perhaps the group of nicely dressed people had just arrived from Durango and were waiting for the stage to Rico. Notice the rough hewn ties placed directly on the ground, the 30-lb rail, and false fronts on some of Rockwood s business establishments. (*Denver Public Library, Western History Department*)

Track layers reached Cascade Siding, mile 478.4, on June 27, 1882, and crews working on the grade had reached Elk Park. There were 500 men working and their salary was $2.25 per day, which was considered good pay for that time.

The most difficult and costly section to build was north of Rockwood. Rockwood Cut, about 350 ft long, required many carefully placed black powder shots to complete. As the track comes out onto the edge of the narrow shelf blasted out of the granite, it still is possible to see the drill holes for the black powder shots. This section, called the High Line, is reported to have cost at least $100,000 per mile to build.

Ernest Ingersoll wrote in the April 1882 *Harper s Magazine* of his first view of the Animas Canyon beyond Rockwood Cut from a rocking stage coach that rattled along the railroad grade:

> Finally we jolt down the last steep declivity, turn a sharp corner and roll out upon the level railroad bed. And what a sight meets our eyes! The bed has been chiseled out of solid rock until there is made a shelf or ledge wide enough for its rails. From far below comes the roar of a rushing stream, and we gaze fearfully over the beetling edge the coach rocks so perilously near...

Although no buildings are left from the busy, bygone construction days, Rockwood is an important station on the D&SNG. During the summer months, the siding is used as a passing track, and the wye often is used by work trains. The beauty of this secluded valley has remained unchanged, however. During Railfests, some excursions originate from here.

NEEDLETON

Needleton was a stop on the Animas Canyon Toll Road. It was also a supply and departure point for prospectors heading up Needle Creek. This station grew in importance when mining in the Needle Mountains and the Chicago Basin area started in the 1880s. A 1969 U.S. Geological Survey report estimated that gold-silver ore from the Needle Mountains amounted to only $12,500. This is far less than the $200,000 newspapers of the day reported.

A description of the Needle Mountains in the December 24, 1887 *The Durango Herald* stated:

> The mountains derive their name from the numerous needle and domelike peaks that rise abruptly out of the surrounding mass of mountains, 10,000 to 12,000 feet in height. These needles and domes are set like mighty watchtowers on the walls of the deep basins to guard the vast treasures hidden away in the great veins beneath. The views obtained from the summits of such of these towers as can be scaled by man, are vast and grand beyond description.

Unfortunately, the "vast treasures" were never found by prospectors.

Remarkably, a post office, which opened in May 1882, lasted until January 31, 1910. Earliest production in Chicago Basin was from hand-sorted gold-silver ore that was carried by pack mules down a steep trail along Needle Creek to the railroad. Mining continued intermittently until about 1917, and was renewed briefly in 1934 after the price of gold increased to $35 an ounce. When the Needle Mountains were designated as part of the Weminuche Wilderness in 1975, all prospecting ceased.

Today, Needleton is a flag stop to let off and pick up fishermen, hikers, and backpackers headed for the incredibly beautiful Needle Mountains and Chicago Basin, where early miners dug for the elusive golden element.

SILVERTON

Unlike Durango, Silverton was an established town when the first train arrived. The first gold lode claim, the Little Giant, was staked in 1870 along a small stream that flows into Arrastra Gulch. When news of this strike reached the outside world, the rush was on. During 1871, an arrastra was built near the Little Giant, and during 1873, the machinery and a boiler for a stamp mill were transported to the mine in pieces on the backs of mules (for additional data on the mines and mineral deposits in the South Silverton Mining District, see pp. 87-88).

Between 1870 and 1875, more miners flocked to Baker's Park and the mining camp growing around the cabin built by miner Francis M. Snowden, Silverton's first resident. By 1875, there were more than 100 buildings in the new town of Silverton; the first school was opened, and postal service started February 1. Also that year the first smelter was built, *The La Plata Miner* published its first issue July 10, and total mineral production for San Juan County reached $101,958. In this age of instant communication, it is difficult to imagine the isolation that must have been a part of spending a winter in these mountains. The May 6, 1876, issue of *The La Plata Miner* gives the following description of the first sign of spring in Silverton:

> Last Tuesday afternoon our little community was thrown into a state of intense excitement by the arrival of the first train of jacks [donkeys], as they came in sight about a mile above town. Somebody gave a shout, 'turn out, the jacks are coming,' and sure enough there were the patient homely little fellows filing down the trail. Cheer after cheer was given, gladness prevailed all around, and the national flag was run up at the post office. It was a glad sight, after six long weary months of imprisonment to see the harbingers of better days, to see these messengers of trade and business, showing that once more the road was open to the outside world.

The year 1876 was important to Silverton for several reasons. San Juan County was carved out of the northern portion of La Plata County, and the town was platted, named, and incorporated. This was also the year Colorado became a state, and the D&RG announced it would build its

77

expanding railroad empire to Silverton. By 1879, a good toll road over Stony Pass was completed, the Melville Reduction Works started operations, and a brick plant produced 12,000 bricks a day. Silverton was becoming a city. The February 1, 1879, *La Plata Miner* contained a long article about mining conditions in the San Juans:

> The country is alive with mining camps containing the richest ores with insufficient capital to work them. Wages are from $1.50 to $4 per day for miners. It requires an apprenticeship to become a good miner as well as a skillful workman about the mines and machinery. Men can work in tunnels and shafts in winter as well as summer. Digging in dirt and rock is hard work.

> The mountains of the San Juan are quite steep, hence miners run tunnels in on the veins, which are much cheaper than sinking shafts. There is plenty of game, but like the mines, requires hunting to find any thing worth having. If women conclude to emigrate, they will push men out of the kitchen and into the mines, where they can dig mineral instead of doing dining room and domestic work about the premises. The wages for women range between $15 and $25 per month. It is cheaper to purchase a good mine than to take the chance of finding one, if one has money.

View northwest of Silverton in 1883. Anvil Mountain is on the skyline.

(W.H. Jackson, Denver Public Library)

An interesting description of Silverton in 1883 appeared in *The Durango Southwest:*

> ...As night darkens, the street scene changes from the work and traffic of the day and assumes quite a festive tone. Sweetly thrilling peals of music are borne upon the night air, and the brilliantly lighted, palatial saloons are thronged by the sportive element, with the pleasure seeking and curious, all classes mingling happily. The sharper with his trap-game laid for the sucker just fresh from the hills with too much dust or bullion certificates, or the greeny from the east with more of the Pop's bond coupons than he has of Ma's wit; either may be enticed by the glowing allurement.

In the rush to finish the Silverton Branch, much trouble and delay was caused because the narrow canyon made it difficult to get ties and rails to the end of the track. But by June 27, the whistle of a D&RG work train was heard for the first time in Silverton. There were then 850 men working on the track, which was 3½ miles from its destination.

Extravagant plans were made to celebrate the arrival of the steel rails in "Silvery Silverton" on July 4. The town was decorated with evergreen boughs, the 14-piece military band from Fort Lewis was to play for the Firemen's Dance. Visitors from as far away as Denver were expected for the Fourth of July celebration.

But once again a railroad celebration was held without the honored "guest" being present. The end of track was still about two miles from Silverton, so visitors and dignitaries on the two excursion trains from Denver were forced to ride in horse-drawn carriages into town.

The celebration included the usual speeches about how the arrival of the railroad would help Silverton, which were followed by rifle, shotgun, and rock drilling contests. Pony, mule, and quarter horse races, and hook-and-ladder teams from nearby towns competed during the afternoon. In the evening, the fireman's dance concluded the day's activities.

On July 8 the construction train arrived, and by July 11 passenger train service commenced. The first ore was shipped on July 13.

The total cost of the Silverton Branch was $575,366.19. Freight rates started at $16 a ton but soon were lowered to $12 a ton. That was quite an improvement over the $60 a ton for pack train service in 1876, or $40 a ton in 1878, or the 58 days it took to bring mining machinery to Silverton over Stony Pass in 1872. In 1882, a first-class ticket from Denver to Silverton cost $37.30. A berth on a Pullman coach was an additional $4.

Silverton was becoming very much a part of the outside world, and it was possible to ride a through train from Silverton to Denver in 29 hours and 50 minutes—if the train was on time.

Silverton was hard hit by the Panic of 1893 when the price of silver plunged from $1.05 per ounce to $0.63 per ounce. Ten large mines in the Silverton mining district closed, and 1,000 men were thrown out of work. Mines that produced some gold and minor amounts of other metals managed to survive that turbulent period.

By 1885, the population of Silverton had grown to approximately 2,000, and Otto Mears' toll road to Ouray was doing a brisk business. Often called the "Pathfinder of the San Juans," Mears decided in 1887 to build railroads instead of toll roads. He was the driving force behind the Silverton Railroad, a short line built to serve the rich mining camps of Chattanooga, Red Mountain, and Ironton, located 18 miles north of Silverton. The narrow gauge rails reached Ironton in the fall of 1888, and the line did a thriving business until 1896, when the richest ores of the Yankee Girl and Guston played out and the mines closed, partly as a result of the Silver Panic of 1893. The line limped along until 1926, when it was dismantled.

Mears' next railroad venture was a line from Silverton to Animas Forks. This railroad, The Silverton Northern, started from Silverton in April 1896 and reached Eureka in June of that year. It wasn't until the early 1900s that the line was extended to Animas Forks. The Silverton Northern continued to operate, sometimes intermittently, until 1942, when the company's three engines were sent to the U.S. Army in Alaska and the track was removed.

The Silverton, Gladstone, and Northerly Railroad was not started by Mears, but in 1913 he took control of the company. The line, just 7½ miles long, ran up Cement Creek to the mining camp of Gladstone. Track laying started in April 1899, and reached Gladstone by July. The line was dismantled in 1938. Map No. 9, p. 62, shows the location of these three lines.

Mears' last railroad venture to the mining camps of the San Juan's was the Rio Grande Southern (see p. 137).

Silverton's economical well-being, like that of most mining camps in Colorado, was influenced by events elsewhere. National financial panics, depressions, wars, weather, and the fluctuating price of metals affected each and every citizen. Through the years, new strikes were made, and companies were organized, sold, reorganized; some went bankrupt. Smelters and concentrating plants were built and operated until the price of concentrates became too low to make a profit. Floods, fires, flu epidemics, labor strikes, accidents, and the difficulties of working at elevations of up to 13,000 feet made mining in the high, rugged San Juan Mountains a real challenge.

In 1959, in an attempt to increase production of known ore reserves of the Sunnyside veins, the American Tunnel was reopened. This tunnel, near the Gold King Mine at Gladstone, found large veins of profitable gold-bearing lead-zinc ores. On June 4, 1971, a major disaster struck when wa-

George L. Beam, the famous official D&RG photographer, captured this interesting view of Greene Street in Silverton. The year is 1910, and the city hall, on the left, is three years old. Sultan Mountain is on the skyline. (Denver Public Library, Western History Department)

ter in Lake Emma seeped down through cracks to an exploratory borehole being drilled about 70 ft below the lake's surface, and soon the entire lake was drained into the mine. The American Tunnel was completely filled with mud. Fortunately, the break occurred on a Sunday, or more than 125 men would have lost their lives. It took two years to clean all the mud from the tunnels and resume mining operations, and the efforts forced the company into bankruptcy. Tragedy occurred again in 1974 when melting snows breached a tailing pond north of Silverton, releasing 100,000 tons of gray slime onto a state highway and into the Animas River above Silverton. This time the cleanup took almost a month and all mining was shut down. In 1985, the company, Standard Metals, sold the Sunnyside mine to Echo Bay Mines. But the new company could not make a profit and shut down all mining in the Sunnyside mine in 1991. San Juan County immediately had the largest unemployment rate of any county in the state.

The National Park Service designated Silverton a National Historical Landmark in 1962. A bronze plaque is mounted on the wall of the old jail. Today, Silverton continues to remember and reflect on its rich mining heritage, even though the town is now largely dependent upon the visitors that arrive each summer day on the D&SNG Railroad.

GEOLOGY

SUMMARY OF ANIMAS CANYON GEOLOGY

The San Juan Mountains contain as great a variety of structures, rocks, minerals, geomorphic features, and magnificent scenery as any mountain range in Colorado. From the oldest Precambrian rocks in the Animas Canyon to the red, oxidized Tertiary volcanic rocks in peaks of the Silverton area, to the glaciated horns of the Needle Mountains, the geology is doubly interesting because of the ease with which these features can be seen.

Geologic events in the Precambrian Era, which ended some 570 million years ago, are much more difficult to decipher and understand than and processes which occurred during the Late Quaternary Period, which began only two million years ago. The major events in each era of geologic time are outlined, and summarized in the Geologic Column, pp. 84-85.

PROTEROZOIC HISTORY

Four major units of Precambrian Period rocks are identified and named in the Animas Canyon. The oldest are ancient, highly metamorphosed gneisses, schists, granite gneisses, and amphibolites of unknown origin. These ancient rocks were folded, faulted, and subjected to extreme heat and pressure during several stages of mountain building. Later they were uplifted and exposed to erosion. The gabbro visible near milepost 475 is a dark, medium- to coarse-grained igneous rock that was intruded (injected or emplaced) into the older gneisses and schists. The third sequence of Precambrian rocks is the Uncompahgre Formation. It is composed of quartzites and conglomerates which were laid down as sand and gravel by rivers upon a newly formed, submerged erosion surface cut on the old gneisses and schists. These Uncompahgre rocks were metamorphosed into hard quartzites, slates, and schists that now are exposed near Elk Park. During late Precambrian time, granitic rocks were injected into the gneisses and schists as hot, fluid masses which gradually cooled into solid granite.

PALEOZOIC HISTORY

At the end of Precambrian Period, the San Juan Mountains were eroded to a rather smooth, rolling plain that was gradually submerged beneath a shallow sea. During Cambrian time, the material brought into this sea by ancient rivers was deposited on the beveled surface of the Precambrian rocks in the form of a thin layer of sandstone and conglomerate that was compacted and cemented into the Ignacio Quartzite. Marine sediments were laid down beneath the sea during the Ordovician, Silurian, and Lower Devonian Periods, but all of these deposits were removed by erosion, leaving only remnants of the Ignacio. Later, the widespread marine Elbert Formation and the Ouray Limestone were deposited above the Ignacio. A time of uplift followed the deposition of the marine Leadville Limestone, as shown by the sporadic distribution of the Leadville, and by its upper surface, which is deeply weathered and which contains sinkholes and caves filled with red muds that later hardened into the Molas Formation.

During the Pennsylvanian Period, thick marine sediments (Hermosa Group) were deposited discontinuously over a long period in the San Juans. Conditions changed early in the Permian Period. Marine limestones and shallow water clastic sediments were no longer deposited, but streams flowing from distant mountains in an ancient desert deposited some 2,500 ft of red conglomerates, shales, sandstones, and siltstones, termed the Rico, Cutler, and the lower part of the Upper Triassic Dolores Formations. The red shales probably formed as clay and silt settled out on the flood plains of sluggish streams that may have drained to southeastern New Mexico and west Texas. The color of these "redbeds" is mainly due to minute amounts of iron hydroxide, which results from the oxidation of iron-bearing minerals. From 3,300 to 4,600 ft of Paleozoic Era sediments were deposited and gradually compacted and cemented into the rocks we find today.

MESOZOIC HISTORY

Mesozoic Era rocks are more than 8,600 ft thick in the area between Durango and Silverton, and consist of alternating marine and nonmarine deposits. The Dolores Formation, part of which is of upper Triassic age, represents a resumption of the "redbed" terrestrial deposition started during the Permian Period. Jurassic rocks consist of nonmarine Entrada Formation, the Wanakah Formation, Junction Creek Sandstone, and the Morrison Formation. The Entrada is a distinctive, massive, cross-bedded white sandstone that was deposited in dunes that had little, if any, vegetation to hold the blowing sand. During the Cretaceous Period, great forests of deciduous trees, which were a source of food for the dinosaurs, grew in abundance and were the source material for most of the thick coal deposits formed during this period. Periodically, ancient seas encroached upon the low land to deposit the marine shales, limestones, marls, and sandstones. The coal beds near Durango formed in lagoons and swamps, and are either above or below these marine sandstones, depending upon whether the sea was advancing or retreating from the land. Toward the end of the Cretaceous Period, 65 million years ago, the region was worn nearly to sea level. At the end of the Cretaceous, the San Juan area was uplifted and the previously deposited sedimentary and igneous rocks were eroded further.

CENOZOIC HISTORY

The modern San Juan Mountains evolved during the Tertiary and Quaternary Periods. During Early Eocene time, some 50 million years ago, the Paleozoic and Mesozoic rocks were bent upward by regional doming so that they now slope away from the center of the dome, the Needle Mountains. The doming probably raised the mountains to at least 10,000 ft above

Geologic Column For Animas Canyon Area

Era	Period	Symbol Used on Maps	Formation Name	Thickness in Feet	Description of Formation
CENOZOIC (Recent Life)	**QUATERNARY**	Qal			Alluvium. Loose rock deposits along stream channels.
		Qg			Pediments and terrace gravels.
		Qls			Landslides. Loose rock and soil from cliffs and slopes above slide.
		Qm			Moraines. Loose rock debris left by retreating glaciers.
		Ended 2 million years ago			
	TERTIARY	Ti	Quartz monzonite stock; dikes of andesite, latite, granite porphyry, and rhyolite		Intrusive volcanic rocks—dikes, sills, batholiths, stocks.
		Tv	Pyroxene-quartz Latite \ Burns quartz Latite \ Eureka Rhyolite } Silverton Volcanic Series	1000 / 1200 / 1800	Extrusive volcanic rocks—flows, tuffs, breccias.
			San Juan Tuff	500	Water-laid tuffs, agglomerates, small flows.
MESOZOIC (Middle Life)	**CRETACEOUS**	*Ended 66 million years ago*			
			McDermott Formation \ Kirkland Shale \ Farmington Sandstone \ Fruitland Formation \ Pictured Cliffs Sandstone	250-300 / 1200 / 350-530 / 200-300	These Upper Cretaceous formations do not appear on any of the guide maps.
		Kmv	Mesaverde Group \ Cliff House Sandstone	300-350	Gray, marine, cliff-forming, calcareous sandstone that weathers to a rusty yellow-brown and red-brown color. Some sandy shale.
			Menefee Formation	125-630	Gray and black shale and cross-bedded sandstone. Coal near top and bottom of formation.
			Point Lookout Sandstone	400	Upper part is buff to white, massive sandstone. Lower part is thin, interbedded sandstones and shales.
		Km	Mancos Shale	1900-2200	Dark gray to black, thin-bedded, marine shale with some limestone and calcareous shale layers.
		Kd	Dakota Sandstone	200	Hard, brown, cliff-forming sandstones, with interbedded carbonaceous shale, conglomeratic sandstone and coal beds.
	JURASSIC	*Ended 144 million years ago*			
			Morrison Formation \ Brushy Basin Member	500	Greenish-gray to maroon bentonitic shale and mudstone interbedded with thin, greenish to gray sandstone beds.
		J	Salt Wash Member		Gray to brown sandstone with some interbedded red to gray shale.
			Junction Creek Sandstone	150	Cliff-forming, white to buff, cross-bedded sandstone with some arkosic sandstone and shale.
			Wanakah Formation	50	Made up of several members consisting of layers of reddish-gray sandstone, shale, and marl. At the base, 2-3' of dark gray to black limestone (Pony Express).
			Entrada Formation	200	White, cross-bedded, massive sandstone.

Geologic Column For Animas Canyon Area

Era	Period	Symbol Used on Maps	Formation Name	Thickness in Feet	Description of Formation
Mesozoic (Middle Life)	UPPER TRIASSIC		Dolores Formation	400-600 near Durango; 40-100 near Ouray	Red, pink, purplish, and gray mudstone, siltstone, shale, and sandstone with fossiliferous conglomerate near base.
PALEOZOIC (Ancient Life)	PERMIAN	R	Cutler "Redbeds"	1900	Dull to purplish red, coarse-grained arkosic sandstones and conglomerates interbedded with fine-grained limy shales, mudstones, and calcareous red shales.
			Rico Formation (or Basal Cutler)	100-165	Red to gray-green to maroon, arkosic sandstone, limestone, and silty claystone.
	PENNSYLVANIAN		*Ended 245 million years ago*		
		Ph	Hermosa Group Honaker Trail Formation	630-680	Interbedded light gray and reddish arkosic sandstones, gray calcareous siltstones, and fossiliferous limestones.
			Paradox Formation	500-1300	Dark gray to black shale, green to brown micaceous sandstone, some siltstone, evaporites, shale, and limestone.
			Pinkerton Trail Formation	0-200	Dark gray siliceous, fossiliferous limestone, and some interbedded gray silty shale.
		Pm	Molas Formation (locally present)	50-100	Red calcareous, fossiliferous shale with limestone and chert nodules. Some sandstone and siltstone. Fills sinkholes in the Leadville Limestone.
	Lower Mississippian		Leadville Limestone (locally present)	100 at Rockwood; thins southward	Light gray fossiliferous limestone with chert nodules, oolite, and some dolomite near base at Rockwood quarry.
	Upper Devonian	D	*Ended 360 million years ago* Ouray Limestone	70 at Rockwood quarry	White to buff to gray limestone and dolomite and some green shale partings.
			Elbert Formation	40-55	Gray, green, red, and purple shale; tan dolomite; red to white siliceous sandstone.
	Upper Cambrian	Ꞓi	*Ended 505 million years ago* Ignacio Quartzite	70 at Baker's Bridge	White, pink, and red fine-grained, thin-bedded quartzite or siliceous sandstone with conglomerate lenses and same sandy shale.
PROTEROZOIC (Before Life)	PRECAMBRIAN	pꞒg	*Ended 570 million years ago* Trimble Granite		Fine-grained gray biotite granite.
			Eolus Granite		Coarse, pink hornblende-biotite granite.
			Whitehead Granite		Reddish-pink biotite granite.
			Tenmile Granite		Pink and gray biotite granite.
			Twilight Granite		Light grayish-pink gneissic granite.
		pꞒu	Uncompahgre Formation	5500	Massive, white or gray quartzite, locally conglomeratic with some dark slate and schist.
		pꞒgb	Gabbro		Medium to very coarse grained intrusive rock that cuts the older gneisses and schists.
		pꞒsg	Ancient granite gneiss, quart-mica schist, amphibolite, gneiss		Finely foliated metamorphic rocks of unknown origin.

the surrounding plains, and is the reason we see successively older rocks dipping beneath the surface as the train goes from Durango to Rockwood.

Starting in Early Oligocene time, the first of three major episodes of volcanism deposited layered eruptive materials totaling almost 1½ miles thick in the San Juan dome. Each period of eruption was followed by subsidence that created the San Juan volcanic depression. Major calderas at Silverton, Lake City, and other sites formed within the older depression. During Late Oligocene time, metallic ore minerals were injected into the fractures, ring dikes, and faults surrounding the calderas.

The transition from the Tertiary to Quaternary Periods was marked by further uplift, faulting and tilting of the mountain mass. Active erosion followed this uplift and produced a mature topography with deep canyons cut through the volcanic rocks sufficiently to expose older sedimentary and igneous rocks. Near the margins of the mountains the streams wandered laterally, cutting extensive erosion surfaces (pediments) that are mantled by thin gravels (Map No. 1, p. 11).

During this time the Pleistocene glacial episodes started. The glaciers of the first stage filled the higher valleys. As the early glaciers receded, the San Juans as we see them today were beginning to take shape. A second episode of glaciation filled the valleys and continued to scour and polish exposed rock surfaces. The last glacial advance filled every major valley in the mountains with ice. The Animas Glacier, the largest in the San Juans, reached as far south as the northern edge of Durango (map, p. 16). This final glacial period left the summit peaks of the Needle Mountains and the

Even after the arrival of the railroad in Silverton, this was the method of getting supplies to the mines in the high country and bringing the ore to Silverton for shipment to the smelters. The pack train is loaded with mine rails for a mine high above treeline.

(Colorado Historical Society)

Grenadier Range as tall, eroded, and serrated horns. The lower slopes were covered with ice and left as smoothed, polished surfaces. The peaks stood from 500 to 1,000 ft above the snowfields. Terminal moraines left by this glacier are found in the low, rounded, hummocky hills near Animas City and as lateral moraines elsewhere in the canyon, particularly where tributary streams join the Animas. After the last of the ice melted, stream erosion continued to carve the valleys into their present form. The Animas River reworked and redeposited the glacial debris and cut a new, deeper channel down through the loose morainal debris in many places. Elsewhere, the river has followed the fractures in the granite and metamorphic rocks to carve deeper channels.

MINING IN THE SOUTH SILVERTON DISTRICT

The Tertiary ore deposits of the South Silverton district, mostly formed within the last 10 million years, occur in veins of a complex fracture zone which roughly mark the southern boundary of the Silverton Caldera. The ring fault zone contains many veins, but most veins were not productive. Map No. 9 (p. 62) shows a generalized view of the ring fault zone, some mineralized faults, and the andesite and latite dikes that vary from a few inches to broad zones 100 ft or more in width. Only a few of the hundreds of mines and prospects can be shown on a map of this scale. The mines at or near the contact of Paleozoic rocks and Tertiary volcanic rocks are replacement-type ore deposits, which means that portions of the rock have been removed by liquids and replaced with ore-bearing minerals.

W.H. Jackson, famous "Picture-Maker of the West," took this photo in 1875 of a prospector's camp on the high slope of Cunningham Gulch east of Silverton. (U.S. Geological Survey)

View looking northwest across Silver Lake (Map No. 9), a cirque lake in a basin formed by glaciers. Elevation of the lake is 12,186 ft, and all supplies and equipment were brought up Arrastra Gulch (in background) to the Silver Lake Mine, first by pack trains and later by wagons and trucks. David J. Varnes, a U.S. Geological Survey geologist, took this photo in 1946 from the location of the Royal Tiger Mine. *(U.S. Geological Survey)*

In 1870 the Little Giant in Arrastra Gulch was the first successful lode mine in the district (mine 13). Gold was ground from the rock in a primitive arrastra; the ore was placed in a circular stone bed, and heavy rocks were dragged across top of the ore by mules or oxen. In 1873 a stamp mill replaced the arrastra, and ore was brought down on the first wire-rope tramway built in the region. Production from the Little Giant peaked in 1873 at $12,000.

The big rush to the San Juans began in 1874 with silver strikes on Hazelton Mountain. Bullion from the Greene and Co. Smelter was shipped to Pueblo via pack train at $60 a ton. Before the arrival of the D&RG, ores worth less than $100 per ton could be not handled profitably.

The Silver Lake mine became a good producer in 1883, as did the North Star on Sultan Mountain, the Belcher, Aspen, Gray Eagle, and North Star on Solomon Mountain, and mines on Green Mountain. The Silver Panic of 1893 caused many mines to close. Later, improved processing methods of low-grade silver, copper, lead, and zind ores kept some mines operating until 1991. Total production of ore in the South Silverton district through 1957 was at least $61 million. Total ore production for all of San Juan County through 1962 was about $135 million.

NATURE

While you are enjoying the sights and sounds of your trip on the narrow gauge and watching steam, smoke, and cinders drift back to the coaches and open cars, take time to also enjoy the magnificent scenery—the mountain peaks, rocks, trees, flowers, and possibly some animals that live in the Animas Canyon.

The plants, mammals and birds found along the route live in distinct communities termed life zones. These zones contain distinctive assemblages of plants and animals that have achieved a balance between local climate and elevation. In Colorado there are six life zones. On your trip today you will traverse two—the foothills, (5,500 ft to 8,000 ft) and the montane, (8,000 ft to 9,500 ft). Major species of trees delineate zonal boundaries; these boundaries are not sharp but merge and overlap each other. Many plants, mammals and birds live in more than one zone.

Within each life zone, various ecosystems comprise specific biological differences. Each ecosystem attracts and supports a wide, but distinct, variety of plants, birds, insects and mammals. Commonly, the north-facing slope of a valley supports a different ecosystem from that found on an opposite south-facing slope.

From a moving train it is almost impossible see the length of the needles or the shape of the cones on different species of conifers. Thus only a few general descriptions are offered that may help identify the different trees. The Mile by Mile Guide® has generalized references to where the different species of trees and a few of the many species of wildflowers occur.

Mammals that live in the Animas Canyon are easily frightened by the sound of the engine and are hard to spot. The best time for seeing some of the larger, more common animals is on late afternoon return trips from Silverton or on the first train to leave Durango in the morning. During the winter runs to Cascade Canyon Wye, elk and mule deer are frequently seen in the lower Animas Valley. Beavers are very common between mile post 482 and Elk Park, and bears are most often seen ambling through the forest in late summer searching for ripe berries.

A new resident to the canyon is a herd of bighorn sheep. During January, 2001 the Colorado Division of Wildlife transplanted 28 bighorn sheep from Georgetown, west of Denver, to the Animas Canyon. The move was made because there were too many sheep for the range to sustain at Georgetown. The last bighorn sheep in the Animas Canyon area died in the 1970s or 1980s, probably because of predators, poaching by man,

Mature bighorn ram.

89

or disease borne by domestic sheep. There are about 70 herds of bighorns scattered throughout the state with a total population of perhaps 7,500.

On a cold, wintry day the sheep were transferred from a truck to a D&SNG boxcar at Rockwood for a ride to Cascade Canyon. Up to 3 ft of snow in the canyon and a derailment in the icy Durango yards combined to keep the "mutinous mutton" in the car. Finally the railroad called out a large maintenance vehicle with a plow and the sheep proceeded to their final destination. Meanwhile, the passenger locomotive was re-railed in Durango and left for Cascade so passengers could witness the unloading.

After the door of the boxcar was opened it took about 30 seconds for the sheep to jump out of the car into the snow and bound up the steep slope on the east side of the track. About 200 passengers and media personnel enjoyed a cold but unforgettable day on the narrow gauge.

The photographs on pp. 92 and 93 are a small sampling of the multitude of animals and wildflowers visible from the train.

Mute deer are common throughout the West.

(National Park Service)

General Characteristics of Trees Along Route

SCRUB OAK

Low growing small tree or shrub with shiny green leaves. Often found growing in dense thickets near Durango. Leaves have rounded lobes.

ROCKY MOUNTAIN JUNIPER

Beautiful, tapered tree about 20 ft tall with olive-green needles divided into tiny segments resembling scales that are flattened against the branchlets. Cones are small bluish berries.

COMMON OR DWARF JUNIPER

Low spreading shrub 2 to 3 ft high. Needles are green, sharp pointed, and awl-like with a white line on upper surface. Prefer open slopes and dry forests, mainly in montane zone.

QUAKING ASPEN

Small to medium-sized tree with small rounded bright green leaves with pointed tips and white bark are called quaking aspens or quakies because the leaves tremble in the slightest breeze. In the fall the leaves turn golden yellow and orange color.

PONDEROSA PINE

Mature trees have an orange-brown bark, an open, rounded crown and may grow to up to 100 ft tall. Often are widely-spaced and form beautiful open park lands on dry slopes near Durango and into the lower mountains.

COLORADO BLUE SPRUCE

Tall stately spruce up to 100 ft tall with green to silver-blue needles that are sharp, stiff and extend from all sides of the twig. Cones hang down. Likes moist lower slopes of canyons and along streams in montane zone.

LODGEPOLE PINE

Tall, slender conifer with yellow-green needles that often are found in dense stands that grow after a forest fire. Otherwise trees are more spreading. Cones are hard and require fire to open and release seed. Prefers montane and subalpine zones.

DOUGLAS FIR

"Christmas tree" shaped evergreen with a pyramidal crown that may reach 100 ft tall. Needles are soft, flat and flexible. Cones hang down. Common in montane zone and on north-facing rocky slopes and shaded ravines.

SUBALPINE FIR

Tall, slender evergreen with a spire-like crown. Needles tend to turn upward. Has smooth grayish-white bark. Cones are purplish-brown color.

ENGLEMANN SPRUCE

Tall, slender evergreen with small light brown cones that hang down. Found in upper montane and subalpine zones. Forms broad belts of dark green forest with subalpine firs. Bark of mature trees is reddish-brown.

LIMBER PINE

Gnarled, rough looking with rounded crown from 30-80 ft tall. with flexible branches and large cones. Likes rocky slopes and ridges of upper montane and subalpine zones.

Mature bull elk sparring at the start of mating season.

Coyote.

Black bear.

Animals, Chase Swift©

Cluster of clematis seed plumes.

Mullein blossom at top of spike.

Flowers, D.B. Osterwald

Yucca in bloom.

Purple fringe.

Rocky Mountain iris.

Fireweed.

Blanket flower.

Porter s aster.

All photographs, D.B. Osterwald

Yarrow.

Indian paintbrush.

Columbine.

Railroading on the Silverton Branch

Introduction

In 1879, William H. Jackson, well-known photographer of the West, had recently completed work for the Hayden Survey and opened a photography studio in Denver. Shortly after, the Denver & Rio Grande Railway commissioned him to photograph the scenery along its rapidly expanding narrow gauge system. The railroad management was so impressed with Jackson's work that he was provided with special trains to use on his assignments. These trains often had a flat car that was used for a camera platform, and a caboose or coach which served as a mobile darkroom. Photographic emulsions were mixed on the spot, the glass plates were hand-coated, and the exposures made while the plates were still wet.

Many priceless early photographs taken along the "Scenic Line of the World" resulted from the association between Jackson and the railroad's advertising department. Jackson first visited the San Juan Mountains in 1873 while taking photographs for the Hayden Expedition, and returned to the region in 1874. His first trip for the D&RG was in October 1880, when the San Juan Extension ended at Osier, Colorado, about 318 miles from Denver and 134 miles east of Durango.

Soon after the track to Silverton was completed, Jackson made a trip over the branch, and for this trip, engine 51, a diamond-stack 2-8-0 named the *South Arkansas*, a caboose, and a flat car were provided. At least five well-known photographs from this trip still exist. All show the engine with a large set of elk antlers mounted on the pilot. Two of the photographs were taken in the Animas Canyon about a mile above Elk Park. Another view is of the train along the river near Needleton, and a fourth is along the High Line. The Jackson photograph on the next page is an unusual view of his photographer's train on the Animas River bridge below Tacoma.

To commemorate the 100th Anniversary of the Silverton Branch, the Intermountain Chapter of the National Railway Historical Society issued a special china plate in July 1982 that features Jackson's 1882 photograph of the High Line.

Jackson's photograph thus sets the stage for a brief history of the Silverton Branch. The following pages include details on the history of the line along with data on operations, locomotives, rolling stock, and other facets of narrow gauge railroading.

Passenger Operations

Although today's schedules accommodate three or more trains departing Durango daily, departure times of the D&SNG trains are not very different from those used by the D&RG in the early 1900s. The D&SNG schedule also doesn't need to coordinate with trains connecting from other

(W.H. Jackson, Colorado Historical Society)

parts of the D&RG system. The last connecting train, the D&RGW's **San Juan**, a daily deluxe train between Alamosa and Durango, was discontinued in January 1951.

In 1886, D&RG passenger train service to Silverton was on the **Silverton Accommodation**, which left Durango at 7:30 a.m. and arrived in Silverton at 12:40 p.m. By 1919, the first class service was on the **San Juan and New Mexico Express**, train Number 115 (westbound) and Number 116 (eastbound). Number 115 left Alamosa at 7 a.m., arrived in Durango, and continued on to Silverton. These same train numbers are used today for the early morning train, the **San Juan Express**.

During D&RGW ownership, train Number 461 to Silverton and train Number 462 to Durango were called the **Silverton Mixed**. These same numbers have been retained by the D&SNG for the **First Silverton Train**. The **Second Silverton Train**, number 463 to Silverton and number 464 to Durango, also have the same numbers at those used by the D&RGW when passenger traffic increased in the 1960s and a second section was needed. Today, the **Third Silverton Train**, Number 465 to Silverton and Number 466 to Durango, handle the ever-increasing number of passengers. These three trains still are listed in the timetable as **Silverton Mixed** trains. The **Cascade Canyon Winter Train**, Numbers 261 and 262, leaves Durango for a 52-mile round trip to Cascade Canyon Wye. Freight may be carried in boxcars just behind the engine.

A few businessmen, miners, and their families rode the Silverton back and forth to Durango and beyond during the first half of the 1900s. Freight trains carried some ore from the Silverton area mines and limestone from the Rockwood quarry to the Durango smelter until it closed in 1930. During World War II the smelter reopened to process vanadium and uranium ore for the Vanadium Corp. of America. Because the ore did not come from the Silverton area, and with no new sources of income, the D&RGW cut back service and wanted to abandon the line. Only heated protests of local residents kept the line open on a reduced schedule, and the mixed trains ran only on Sundays, Wednesdays, and Fridays.

After the war, railfans and railroad club members began using the line for narrow gauge excursion trains—an experience very different from riding cross-country troop trains during the war! Promotion of these trips were largely due to the efforts of railfans and Rio Grande conductor Alva Lyons. During those early years a caboose was also available for passengers and the conductors came through the train with coffee brewed on the stove of the caboose.

These trips did much to publicize the San Juan Extension and the San Juan mountains and ridership gradually increased. In 1947 the D&RGW built a glass-roofed observation car, the Silver Vista, that allowed amazing 180° views from the train. Unfortunately, a 1953 shop fire in Alamosa destroyed this unique car.

Alva Lyons (1897-1990) served many years as a D&RGW conductor in Durango. On August 3, 1991, a memorial plaque in his honor was unveiled at the Durango depot. It reads: *"His career with the D&RGW spanned 51 years from 1915 to 1966. His vision and perseverance were important factors in saving the Silverton Branch from abandonment in the 1950s. He offered coffee, information, and tall tales to mid-century tourists, increasing ridership and winning friends from around the world."*

Amos Cordova retired from the railroad in 1998 after 47 years of service on the D&RGW and as Vice President of Marketing and Public Relations for the D&SNG starting in 1981. He came to Durango in 1962 as station agent. Under the leadership of Alexis McKinney, Amos helped direct the development of Rio Grande Land in the mid-1960s. His wife Julie worked as cashier in the depot for 22 years. Together they offered friendship and help to all. Amos now stays busy with photography and painting, and also serves on the Durango City Council.

The glass-roofed Silver Vista *observation car on the end of a passenger train waiting to depart the Durango depot in 1947, soon after its construction. This is very likely the same excursion train pictured below.* *(John W. Hand)*

On a railfan trip in August 1947, the northbound train stopped after crossing the Animas River below Tacoma to let passengers off for a photo run-by. All the cars except the Silver Vista *were painted Pullman green. Car 126 is behind the engine, followed by combine 212.* *(Colorado Historical Society)*

The Farmington branch was built to standard gauge in 1905 to Farmington, New Mexico. The D&RG anticipated that this outlet to the south would connect with other railroads in New Mexico and carry coal from the San Juan Basin to smelters in New Mexico and Arizona. This grand scheme never materialized, and the "Red Apple Line" was converted to narrow gauge in 1923 and carried shipments of fruit, farm, and ranch products. A major oil and gas boom in the San Juan Basin (the area around Farmington) during the 1950s extended the life of the San Juan Extension by almost 20 years. In fact, during 1955, the Farmington branch had the highest number of car loadings of the entire D&RGW system.

Farmington branch motive power: standard gauge 4-6-0 No. 510 in Durango on June 2, 1923. The large smokestack in the background is part of the Durango smelter.

A westbound stock train pulled by 482 on the Farmington branch south of Carbon Junction. Oct. 25, 1946. (Both photos, Otto C. Perry, Denver Public Library, West. History Dept.)

Photographer and D&RG general car foreman Monte Ballough recorded this scene of Durango looking northwest toward Perins Peak sometime between 1910 and 1920. At this time, the Durango yards were dual gauge (three rails) to accommodate the Farmington branch. *(Collection of Margaret Ballough Palmer)*

View northwest from the hill overlooking the Durango yards. Engine 484 was assembling a work train headed for Flora Vista, New Mexico, to repair a washout on the Farmington branch. June 28, 1966. *(F.W. Osterwald)*

In May 1967, the double-spout water tank in the Durango yards was torn down, and in April 1968, the coaling tower was demolished to make way for highway construction. Resulting track realignments gave the Durango yards a new look in 1968. Later, the car shed was removed and D&RGW carmen could no longer work indoors.

*To illustrate these changes, compare this photo with those on p. 99. By May 1968, the new loop to turn **The Silverton** trains cut across the yard track, putting a sharp reverse curve in the track leading to the roundhouse that made access difficult for engines.*

(Both photos, F.W. Osterwald)

D&RGW K-27 engine 453 heading north at the south switch of the Hermosa siding, probably in the early 1950s. K-27 engines were equipped with these full-size wedge plows for snowplowing in the narrow confines of the Animas canyon.

(Collection of Kenneth Logan)

*D&RGW **San Juan** narrow gauge passenger equipment sitting on dual gauge track in the Alamosa yards, 1939. Many of these coaches are still used today on the D&SNG.*

(Turner Van Nort)

The Rio Grande Southern Railroad was dismantled in 1952, and in 1962 the D&RGW petitioned the U.S. Interstate Commerce Commission (ICC) to abandon the Silverton Branch, but the petition was denied largely because of the increasing value of the line as a tourist attraction.

Early in 1963 the Rio Grande purchased a number of buildings and land near the depot and began a renovation program called "Rio Grande Land." Stores, gift shops, the General Palmer Hotel, and the Grande Palace Restaurant were opened, and a large parking lot was built on the west side of the depot. As ridership continued to increase, new coaches were built in Denver, and a second section of **The Silverton** was added in 1963.

A petition to abandon the route between Farmington, Durango, and Alamosa was filed with the ICC in 1967, and final approval was granted in 1969. The last run over the line in December 1968 was a westbound train to Durango pulled by the 473 that included dead K-36 number 481 and several passenger coaches.

Because of the intensive efforts of many people and organizations, the states of Colorado and New Mexico banded together in July 1970 to purchase 64 miles of track between Antonito, Colorado and Chama, New Mexico and a large amount of equipment, buildings, and rolling stock. This portion of the line is now known as the Cumbres & Toltec Scenic Railroad. The other 110 miles of track to Chama and the Farmington branch were dismantled, and the remaining rolling stock sold or burned.

The last run on the Farmington branch. K-36 No. 483 leaving Durango, August 31, 1968, for Carbon Junction, where it picked up a train of oil field supplies. A relocation of U.S. Highway 160 later buried this portion of the yards. *(Al Chione)*

Throughout the 1960s and 1970s, the D&RGW attempted to find a buyer for the Silverton Branch. On March 25, 1981, Charles E. Bradshaw Jr., of Orlando, Florida, paid $2.2 million in cash for this last remaining vestige of the once-extensive D&RGW narrow gauge system. Included in the sale were the steam locomotives, rolling stock, work equipment, and buildings that remained in Durango and along the line to Silverton. Also, several locomotives stored in the Alamosa roundhouse were sold and transported to Durango (see p. 129).

Extensive engineering studies of the roadbed, track, bridges, and structures determined that by widening some rock cuts and strengthening some bridges, larger and heavier locomotives could be used over the entire line. In August 1981, newly refurbished engine 481 was the first K-36 to operate north of Rockwood.

Winter trips between Durango and Cascade Canyon, which run November through April, grow in popularity every year. This scene is just north of the Animas River bridge at mile 452.4.   *(©Robert Royem Photography)*

A new car shop was erected on the site of the one torn down by the Rio Grande, and three stalls and a welding shop were added to the Durango round-house by December 1984. Also during the summer of 1981, the Cascade Canyon Wye was added at mile 477.5. During the off-season winter months, round-trip trains operate only to this point, which allows the railroad to continue passenger service year-round without having to keep the upper Animas River canyon unblocked from the numerous snowslides.

In March 1997 Charles Bradshaw sold the D&SNG to First American Railways, Inc., a publicly-held corporation headquartered in Hollywood, Florida, and in July 1998 the railroad was sold again to American Heritage Railways with headquarters in Coral Gables, Florida.

The American Heritage Railways Corporation officers, President Allen C. Harper, Vice President and Chief Operating Officer Jeffery D. Jackson, and Vice President for Marketing Kristi Nelson Cohen, began planning new activities and special events for the railroad (see pp. 160-163).

The company converted eight stalls of the Durango roundhouse into a marvelous railroading museum (photo, p. 15). In 1999 the Silverton depot and freight yards also opened as a museum, and the Cascade Canyon Wye pavilion was completed (photo, p. 42).

In addition to the D&SNG Railroad, American Heritage Railways also owns and operates the **Great Smoky Mountains Railroad**, with offices in Dillsboro, North Carolina. Steam and diesel trains operate through the scenic mountains of western North Carolina along the southern border of Great Smoky National Park.

The "5 Star Award for Best Attraction" was awarded to the D&SNG by the National Association of Travel Journalists in 1998, and the Society for American Travel Writers designated the train as one of the "Top 10 Most Exciting Train Journeys in the World."

WEATHER

Keeping the lines open across Cumbres Pass and on the Silverton Branch through long winter months was more than a challenge for early-day railroaders. The winter of 1884 was one of the worst on record for Colorado. Snow started falling in the San Juans February 2 and continued for 20 long days. By February 9th, there were 3 ft of snow on the ground in Silverton and drifts were up to 7 ft deep. Other storms followed, and the railroad was blocked for 73 days. Finally in March, after the line was opened to milepost 492, a pack train was sent down the Animas Canyon to meet a work train and brought badly needed supplies to town. But it was April 16 before a train arrived in Silverton with two cars of merchandise, three cars of coal, two of grain and hay, and some fresh meat.

After the disastrous winter of 1884 and another severe winter in 1886, Silverton repeatedly petitioned the railroad to build snowsheds and keep snow removal equipment in Silverton so work trains would not have to buck snow while climbing the grade. Only one snowshed was built (at mile 492.45), and work equipment never was kept in Silverton. During normal winters, well-known avalanche areas always ran, carrying tons of snow to the bottom of the canyon and blocking the track for weeks. During these times, baggage, mail, and passengers had to be transferred by foot or burros to stub trains on the north side of particularly long, deep snowslides.

In 1886, the line was closed for four weeks because of snowslides and in 1891, Silverton was isolated for 51 very long days. Also in 1891, avalanches came down Kendall Mountain and spread out on the flat ground near the south end of Silverton. Opening the track during these blockades was a backbreaking job, and laborers earned only $1.40 per day to shovel out snowslides by hand. During the winter of 1905, many trains were delayed and cancelled. One snow blockage in February 1905 lasted three weeks, and was followed in March and April by both melting snow and heavy, wet spring snowstorms which caused a rash of derailments. In addition, many mudslides covered the track during the spring thaw.

Throughout the early months of 1906, the D&RG was almost completely blocked between Antonito and Silverton. By March, Cumbres Pass finally was opened and men and equipment were transferred to the Silverton Branch, where 11 miles of snowslides needed clearing. Snow was so deep in the upper canyon that it was shoveled into coal cars so they could be pulled out of the canyon and the snow dumped. To get through the largest of the slides, railroad officials decided to simply tunnel through the mass of ice, rocks, and shredded timber. This snow tunnel received a great deal of publicity and it was suggested that the Rio Grande offer special excursion rates for rides through the unusual tunnel. On April 16, 1906, the first train in 34 days finally entered Silverton.

In April 1906, when crews had just about finished the backbreaking job of tunneling through the huge slide near the snowshed, the Rio Grande sent official photographer George L. Beam to record some of the work in opening the Silverton Branch. This may have been the first engine to start through the tunnel. The white flags on the engine indicate that it is an extra train.

The first scheduled southbound freight train through the snow tunnel. There are no flags on the head engine. The brakemen are standing on the top of the cars, ready to club down the hand brakes if necessary. (Both photos, George L. Beam)

Perhaps this view looking south is of the rear of the freight train shown in the photo at the bottom of the previous page. Some melting appears to have occurred, because the roadbed is dry. One may assume the men were relieved that their labors were over—at least for a few days. (George L. Beam, from glass plate negatives in the D&RGW collection,

courtesy Jackson C. Thode)

View northward of the interior of the 1906 snow tunnel.   (Collection of W.D. Joyce)

During 1908, snowfall was very heavy, and in March it was reported that water two feet deep was running *through* the snowshed. Snowfall was the heaviest in many years, and all railroads out of Durango were blocked in January. Cumbres Pass was closed January 24, cleared by the 26th, only to be blocked again three days later. As if that wasn't enough trouble for the D&RG, the Rio Grande Southern (RGS) rotary plow broke down and had to be taken to Alamosa for repairs. The Rio Grande rotary that normally worked on Marshall Pass had to be brought to Ridgway to open the RGS, working southward. On February 11, the *Durango Democrat* stated that the Silverton Branch would be open shortly—but it wasn't until February 26 that a train finally arrived in Silverton. On March 7, another huge slide came down near Elk Park and blocked the track, causing passengers to walk across the slide to a stub train from Silverton.

Other years when snowslides blocked the Silverton Branch were 1916, 1928, and 1932. In 1932, the job of opening the line seemed almost hopeless, so the work of clearing the track was suspended from February to May. By that time Silverton was less dependent upon the railroad for all supplies, food, and coal because Highway 550 was kept open. After 1964, if the main line from Alamosa was blocked by drifts and snowslides, the Rio Grande simply closed all operations and waited for the spring thaws.

The narrow confines of Animas Canyon make the Silverton Branch susceptible to devastating floods. Heavy rains in September 1909 caused extensive washouts, and in 1911, another flood effectively blocked the branch for 63 days. The Rio Grande paid more than $10,000 in wages to laborers who worked to open the line. Some of the rail washed into the river channel in 1911 still is visible. Flooding occurred again in 1927 and

View of the D&RG track at Tacoma that was washed out after the 1911 flood. Additional photographs are on p. 39. *(Colorado Historical Society)*

First mixed train going through the Garfield slide in February 1943 after it was cleared. That year the slide was 75 ft deep and about 500 ft long. Combination car 212 is ahead of the caboose. *(Colorado Historical Society)*

caused the Animas River to move into a new channel in the canyon near Needleton. The original Needleton siding had to be moved to its present location, and nearly two miles of the railroad between mileposts 481 and 483 were relocated.

On September 4, 1970, light rain began to fall in the mountains around Silverton. It continued for three days as a heavy downpour. A total of 4.19 inches fell on Silverton. High water in Mineral Creek roared into the lower portions of Silverton, knocked out the new sewage treatment plant, and destroyed the Mineral Creek campground, along with many local roads. The water supply system for Silverton was badly damaged, and water covered the lower end of Silverton for about a day and a half.

Private property hardest hit by this flood was the D&RGW railroad. From a point just south of Tacoma and north all the way to Silverton, parts of the track either were badly damaged or entirely destroyed. Gauges for measuring water flow at Tacoma were washed away; this also happened in the earlier floods.

Fortunately, no bridges on the Silverton Branch were destroyed in 1970, although small bridges over the tributary streams emptying into the Animas were badly clogged with debris. Only the U.S. Forest Service bridge at Cascade Creek was destroyed. Hardest hit were sections of track between Tacoma and Tank Creek, in the Cascade Creek area, at Tefft, and at Elk Park (photo, p. 39). In these locations, the track was completely removed from the roadbed. The D&RGW started repairs as soon as the water receded. This work continued until snow drove the repair crews out of the canyon. But by November, speeders could run over all 45 miles of track and most of the railroad was in excellent shape for opening day, May 29, 1971. Slow orders were in effect at some places for a few weeks until the new roadbed had settled and stabilized.

Durango escaped serious damage in the 1970 flood. The Animas valley just north of the city resembled a large lake for a while, but the area is a natural reservoir for high water of the river, and no extensive damage was done except to some roads, bridges, and water systems.

This photo was taken near Tacoma, on September 10, 1970, four days after flood waters receded. The extensive damage to the roadbed and track are graphically illustrated as this section has been lifted off the roadbed and left in the stream channel.   (R.W. Osterwald)

The infamous Snowshed slide at mile 492.5 did its usual job of making the work of opening the line to Silverton a real challenge in 1995. This southward view was taken while D&SNG crews, using front end loaders, removed snow from the track. Contrast this operation with that used in 1905-06 as shown on pp. 106-107.

(Andrew Councill, Durango Herald*)*

THE DURANGO ROUNDHOUSE

From the time it was erected in 1881, no major modifications to the original 10-stall Durango roundhouse were made until June 1965 when stalls 4, 5, and 6 (numbered from east to west) were enlarged to allow the K-36 and K-37 engines to fit completely inside. In 1971, after the end of freight service, stalls 7, 8, 9, and 10 were removed, the roof was replaced, and stalls 1, 2, and 3 were converted into a machine shop. In 1985 the D&SNG replaced the four missing stalls.

This photo from the late 1930s, shows the original roundhouse and the 65-ft turntable that came from Alamosa in 1924 and replaced the 50-ft original. Note the K-36 in stall 5 that is sitting partly outdoors.   *(Denver Public Library, Western History Department)*

A summer view of the roundhouse and turntable taken in the 1950s when the narrow gauge still ran freight across Cumbres Pass and to Farmington, N.M. Number 492 is moving off turntable into a stall, and the wedge plow is ready to be installed on one of the K-27 engines when winter arrives, as shown in the photo on p. 101.   *(Colorado Historical Society)*

The scene that greeted firemen and D&SNG employees after fire was discovered in the roundhouse. *(Photo ©Paul Connor)*

During the early morning of February 10, 1989, a night security guard discovered a fire in the southeastern corner of the roundhouse machine shop behind a kiln which spread rapidly and quickly destroyed the entire building. All six operable engines were in the roundhouse, and at first it was feared all were damaged beyond repair.

Temperatures near the roof of the roundhouse were estimated to have reached 2,500 to 3,000°F, and collapsed onto the engines causing extensive damage. The intense heat burned all the paint off the engines, so repainting became a priority to prevent corrosion. The machine shop was totally destroyed, along with many spare parts that are no longer available. Engine 473 suffered the worst damage.

One week later, the debris had been cleaned out, and a temporary machine shop was assembled outdoors along the west wall of the roundhouse and the roundhouse crew began repairs. Fortunately the winter weather turned mild and working outside was not a problem.

Exactly one year after the fire, a new 36,000-sq ft roundhouse and machine shop complex was dedicated. Inside are now seven engine stalls, eight new locomotive storage stalls, and a machine shop with a total of 27 new machines including a 20-ton traveling crane and a Craven quartering machine obtained from the South African Railroad. The total cost of the new facilities exceeded $2 million.

Engines 476 (left) and 473 (right). The 473 suffered the worst damage because it was closest to the source of the fire and because the loaded tender burned. The steam dome was damaged, and the cab was totally destroyed. 473 had been completely overhauled prior to the tragedy and was ready for operation. *(Erick Nelson)*

Engine 476, here in stall number one, was the first to be returned to service. It made a test run April 13 to Cascade Canyon Wye, pulling seven empty coaches. As this train left Durango, it passed under crossed ladders of the Durango Fire Department. *(©Paul Connor)*

April 7, 1989. At the time of the fire, 481, at left, had no boiler jacket, lagging, or flues, and both the smokebox front and firebox doors were open, which helped to cool the boiler. Engine 478, right, has just been painted.

This photograph illustrates how much was accomplished in less than two months time. From left to right are engines 481, newly-painted 478, 497, 476 (behind the Pettibone machine), and 480. *(Both photos, F.W. Osterwald)*

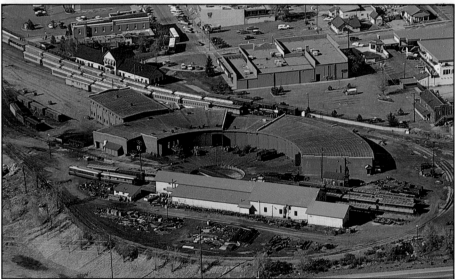

These photos, taken from Smelter Mountain in May 1989 (top) and May 1990 (bottom), show the walls of the destroyed original roundhouse and the new locomotive facility that replaced it just a year later.   (Both photos, Ed Boucher, courtesy D&SNG Railroad)

OPERATING PROCEDURES

Dispatching trains is a highly developed method of directing train movements by the use of very specific rules, timetables and train orders which were sent by skilled Morse telegraphers from a centralized dispatch office to station operators along the route. The operators then related those orders to the train crew using written forms called "flimsies" (p. 159) because they were printed on thin paper. The D&SNG used the old D&RGW flimsy and clearance card system until 1986. The first trackside signals on American railroads were various types of indicators that told the crew if orders were to be received ahead. No trackside signals have ever been on the Silverton Branch.

In 1981 a modern radio communication system was installed on the D&SNG and a dispatcher began to work in the Durango yard for the first time in more than 30 years. In 1986 the D&SNG began operating on a 'track warrant control' system. Similar systems are used by mainline railroads throughout the United States to control train movements over a given section of track. The dispatcher issues a track warrant by radio to employ-

D & R G W Form 3250
Sec. 8

DENVER NOV 30   62
                                                          19

TRAIN ORDER NO. 315

To C&E ENG 483

At CHAMA   X.   Opr.   M.

ENG 483 RUN EXTRA CHAMA TO DURANGO

ENG 480 RUN EXTRA DURANGO TO GATO HAS RIGHT OVER EXTRA 483

WEST DURANGO TO GATO HELP EXTRA 483 WEST GATO TO MP 443

THEN RUN EXTRA MP 443 TO DURANGO

HWE

Chief Dispatcher

CONDUCTOR, ENGINEMAN AND REAR TRAINMAN MUST EACH HAVE A COPY OF THIS ORDER.

Made   Time 818   M.   Opr.

A 1962 D&RGW train order for the narrow gauge.   *(Collection of R. W. Osterwald)*

117

ees needing to use a section of track between designated points, such as stations listed in the timetable. Scheduled trains operate on the rights of the railroad timetable. All other movements on the D&SNG, including track maintenance cars and light engines, require permission via a track warrant from the Durango dispatcher.

Other operating rules have remained unchanged for over a hundred years. For example, hand and lamp signals are still used.

To ensure the safety of the traveling public and the employees, operating rules on the D&SNG are as strict as on any standard gauge mainline railroad. Flags by day and marker lights by night on the locomotive and the rear car serve important functions. The locomotive of a regularly scheduled train, with no following section, carries no flags or lighted classification lamps. The locomotive of the first section of a multi-section train carries green flags by day and green lamps by night. Any additional sections of

Hand and Lamp Signals.

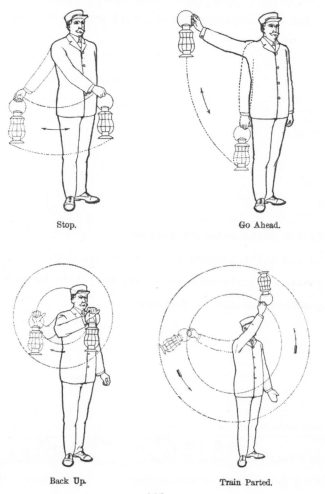

Stop.

Go Ahead.

Back Up.

Train Parted.

the same train carry no color signals. The purpose of these flags is to inform opposing rail traffic, encountered en route, of the presence of the following sections so as to ensure safe track movements (photo, p. 125).

A yellow flag placed on the engineer's side of the rail, indicates that the track ahead is under a speed restriction. Speed restrictions are also given by radio in association with the track warrant system (a red flag or lamp placed anywhere on the track ahead is a stop signal and may not be passed without proper authority). A blue metal sign (or blue flag) placed at the entrance to a track or on the engine, indicates that workers are under the train or around it. If a train is protected by a blue signal it must not be coupled onto or moved, and only the employee who placed the blue flag is authorized to remove it.

Motorists arriving in Durango in the late afternoon or evening usually become aware of the D&SNG as each of several trains whistle loud and long for road crossings. The D&RGW narrow gauge used a wide range of locomotive whistle types that were unmatched by many larger railroads. The tones ranged from the beautiful five-chime whistles on the 480s to the lower toned homemade chime whistles on the 490s, or the hoarse-sounding Alco passenger whistles on the 470s. Occasionally a passenger chime whistle from a long-gone standard gauge engine would turn up on a narrow gauge engine. In earlier years, D&RGW locomotives regularly assigned to freight service were typically equipped with a single-chime or occasionally a three-chime whistle, while passenger locomotives were equipped with a five-chime whistle. Eventually, standards were eased and various whistle types were installed on many engine classes.

Federal railroad safety laws require whistles and bells on locomotives. The bell is rung as a warning when the train is about to make a movement, or when it is approaching a station. A locomotive whistle is not just a noisemaker; it is used to broadcast warnings to bystanders and to inform employees as to movements the train will be making. The most common whistle signals are on the inside front cover.

The track switches (or turnouts) in use today are different from the original ones. The old type, called stub switches, were simply devices that moved the running rails from one position to another. Today's switches consist of fixed running rails with a pair of knife-shaped tapered points that can be moved from one side to the other between the rails. A switch stand is located at each track switch. A vertical steel rod with a handle that is connected to a crank pushes a rod between the ties to move the switch points from one side to the other. On top of the vertical rod is a green metal diamond, and directly below is a round, red metal target placed at right angles to the diamond. The engineer or

fireman will see the green diamond if the switch is aligned for the normal route, or the red circle if it is aligned for the diverging or side track.

Milepost

During your trip you probably will notice a number of small trackside signals, in addition to the switch stands. Most important (at least on your trip today!) are the mileposts. Their history and use are described on page 8 and are illustrated on the back cover.

Raise Flanger

Road engines on wintertime passenger trains are normally equipped with snowplows on their pilots. If there has been a heavy snow storm, sometimes a small car called a flanger will be coupled behind the engine of an extra work train. The flanger has two blades on either side that are raised and lowered by air pressure from the locomotive. The blades push the snow from the track and cut grooves in ice and snow just inside the rails to give clearance for wheel flanges. The small black triangle with two horizontal lines tells the engineer to raise the flanger blades while proceeding through crossings.

Other signals tell the engineer when to whistle for a road crossing. Yard Limits, a specific type of main track authority as prescribed by the operating rules, are marked by signs with two blades angled upward. These can be seen near Durango and Silverton.

Crossing

Whistle

Yard Limit

TRACK

Without well-built and maintained track and roadbed, your ride today would be rough—and unsafe. The engineering departments of all railroads keep records, called track profiles, that are graphic representations of a particular section of track. Track profiles are used by dispatchers and other railroad officials to determine the types of engines and cars that can be used on different parts of the line, where helper engines are required, where passing tracks and sidings are located, and where locomotives can get water. Maximum curvature and grade profiles dictate the amount of trailing tonnage allowed on trains and also how much locomotive tractive effort is needed to negotiate the grade. The weight and type of rail also must be taken into account, so that heavy engines are not allowed to travel on sections with light rail.

Track for the D&RG Silverton Branch originally was laid with light steel rail from the Colorado Coal and Iron Co. at Pueblo which weighed 30 lb per yard. This was the first steel rail produced at the Pueblo plant.

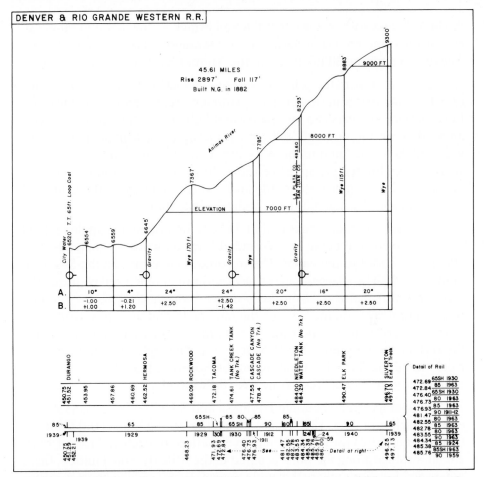

Profile of the Silverton Branch. Circles indicate where water is available. Line A gives the maximum curvature between points, and line B gives the maximum grade. Since this profile was prepared, all 65-lb rail has been replaced with 85- and 90-lb rail. (Jackson C. Thode)

Ties were untreated native timbers that were rough-hewn, not sawed. For the most part, ballast was absent. It is quite likely that the railroad considered such things as ballast and level track to be luxuries that could be purchased later with operating revenues. No tie plates were used; the rails were spiked directly to the ties. The resulting railroad bed was adequate for the light engines and cars that were used during the early years. This track work was inexpensive, but the grade on which it was laid was not. Much of it, particularly in the Animas Canyon, was blasted from solid rock. Today's sawed and creosoted ties are quite sophisticated compared to the untreated axe-hewn ties of the 1880s (photos, p. 75, 123).

Between 1911 and 1917, most original rail was replaced by 40- and 52-lb rail so that the heavier 450-series engines could be used on the line. Between Durango and Rockwood 57- and 65-lb rail was used up to the time

121

the branch was sold in 1981. All D&SNG track is now 85- and 90-lb rail except for some 65-lb rail between the Durango depot and 32nd Street. The only remaining 30-lb rail lies in the Animas River as a result of floods.

As noted on p. 6, the principle reason the D&RG was built to a gauge of 3 feet was that a narrower gauge is much less expensive to construct. Locomotives and cars can be smaller and lighter, and thus could be operated safely on the original 30-lb rail. Building track with sharper curves was well-suited for mountainous terrain. Unfortunately, the light rail and sharp curves limited the speed of trains. Slow schedules and the expense of transferring freight to standard gauge cars brought about the demise of nearly all narrow gauge railroads in the United States.

Railroad curves are measured in degrees, describing the angle marked at the center of the curve by two radial lines drawn from the ends of a 100 ft-long chord to the curve. The maximum curvature on the Silverton branch is 24°. The sharpest curves have additional railed spiked inside the running rails (photo, p. 28) to keep the car wheels close to the running rails, prevent wear on the sides of the rail heads, and prevent spreading of the rails, all of which could cause a derailment. The sharp curves are also the reason the 490-series locomotives, with their relatively rigid trailing truck design, had trouble running on the Silverton branch and are better suited to the gentler curves on the C&TS Railroad.

The average grade between Hermosa and Silverton is 2.5%, as shown on the track profile, p. 121. This is called the 'ruling grade' and it means that the track rises (or falls) 2.5 feet in elevation for each 100 feet of horizontal distance along the rail. As noted in the Mile By Mile Guide®, there are several locations where the grade exceeds 2.5%, such as short stretches of nearly 4% grade in the Animas Canyon past Needleton near milepost 488. Although a 2.5% grade is somewhat steep as compared to most standard gauge railroads, it is gentle compared to the continuous 4% grade on the west side of Cumbres Pass on the C&TS Railroad out of Chama, New Mexico. The D&SNG formerly pulled the maximum number of cars an engine could handle upgrade, but the addition of more trains has allowed the loads to be lightened by a car or two.

The original bridges were wooden. Most of the timbers and the iron for these bridges were fabricated in Cañon City, and shipped to Durango. The D&RG built these bridges as rapidly as possible knowing they would have to be replaced with sturdier ones in the future. All original bridges have been replaced with modern ones of either steel or treated wood construction. In addition, many larger trestles have been filled in so that less maintenance is required, and greater speeds and loadings are possible. A large curved trestle at mile 470.2 burned in 1904 and was replaced by a fill of crushed rock (photo p. 33).

This rare photograph, probably taken in late 1882 or early 1883, shows the view southeast across Lightner Creek toward the San Juan and New York Smelter on the south side of the Animas River. After crossing the river via the lightweight pony truss bridge on the left, the track in the foreground led to some coke ovens (not visible to the right) and then looped back to the smelter. The RGS also used this bridge from 1890 until 1893 when a two-span Howe truss structure replaced it.   *(Durango Public Library)*

The bridge and building yard of the D&RG in Cañon City, Colorado, in 1882. Bridge timbers were prepared here for use on all portions of the system. The boxcar stands on light rail, fastened to rough-hewn, unballasted ties.   *(Colorado Historical Society)*

LOCOMOTIVES

A hundred years ago, passenger and freight trains, powered by steam locomotives, were the main form of transportation and a necessary—and somewhat romantic—part of every day life in America. For many passengers this will be a new and exciting experience to ride behind a steam locomotive and watch it pull your train into the mountains and wind back and forth along the Animas River with steam and smoke billowing from the smokestack. You may be surprised to learn that the D&RGW narrow gauge system west of Alamosa was the last 100% steam-operated railroad in North America. Today the 45-mile route of the D&SNG and the 64-mile C&TS are all that remain of the San Juan Extension built between 1879 and 1882 to reach the mining camps and towns in southwestern Colorado.

Water and coal are carried in the tender, which is connected behind the engine. Coal is shoveled from the tender through the firebox door inside the engine cab. Heat from the fire passes through dozens of flues in the boiler, which is the part of the engine ahead of the firebox extending to the smokebox. The flues are surrounded by water that has been forced against steam pressure into the boiler with a steam-powered injector. The heat is transferred to the water, and the water is converted into steam.

It takes many hours to steam up a cold locomotive, during which time the boiler parts expand. Unless this is done slowly and gradually, the boiler steel may be damaged. It is for this reason that engines are kept "steamed up" or "alive" after the day's run is completed. In fact, a locomotive can be kept hot continuously except for a day or two a month for inspection and boiler cleaning, and of course whenever boiler repairs are needed.

Live steam from the top of the boiler is fed through the throttle valve inside the steam dome, which is the highest point in the boiler, through a series of tubes called the superheater, then to two cylinders, one on each side of the engine, ahead of the drive wheels (drivers). These cylinders, which are similar to the cylinders in an automobile engine, contain movable pistons that are connected to the main rods which connect to the drive wheels. Valves with adjustable travel control the admission of steam to the ends of the cylinders. The engineer's reverse lever changes the horizontal position of the valves with respect to the pistons, so that more or less steam is admitted to the cylinders as required, thereby causing the engine to use steam more efficiently or to move in the reverse direction.

The steam actually follows a convoluted path from the steam dome to the cylinders. Inside the steam dome is saturated steam with its temperature near the boiling point of water. Leaving the throttle valve through a large pipe, saturated steam then enters a collection of smaller pipes via a large header that run into and then out of the flues. These pipes and the header are called the superheater unit, a device invented in 1894 that can

124

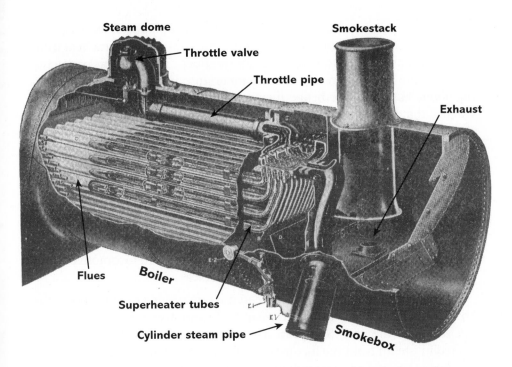

Steam dome

Throttle valve

Smokestack

Throttle pipe

Exhaust

Flues

Boiler

Superheater tubes

Cylinder steam pipe

Smokebox

A cutaway view of a superheated locomotive boiler illustrating the major internal parts.

Silverton, Colorado, on May 6, 1989, after the arrival of the second section of the First Silverton Train (number 461), pulled by engine 497. Green marker flags on engine 476 indicate that a second section was following (one of the marker flags was lost before reaching Hermosa). More on the use locomotive flags and marker lights is on p. 118. Note how much smaller the K-28s are compared to the much larger K-37s, and the air compressor on the smokebox front of number 476. (Ren Osterwald)

increase locomotive efficiency by at least 15%. A superheater increases the temperature of the steam to 600°F or greater by extracting extra heat from the hot exhaust gases moving through the flues. The amount of energy stored in the steam increases as the temperature increases above the boiling point. Thus the superheater increases efficiency by using heat from the exhaust that would otherwise be wasted.

Steam expands in the front of one cylinder, driving the piston and main rod backward, and also expands in the rear of the cylinder on the other side of the engine, driving that piston and rod forward. This backward and forward motion of the rods against the crankpins on the drivers forces the wheels to turn. The steam expanding against one side of the piston also forces spent steam on the opposite side out of the cylinders and up the stack along with smoke from the burning coal. This exhausted steam makes the unforgettable sound that is so characteristic of steam locomotives: four exhaust sounds for each revolution of the drivers.

In addition to producing superheated steam needed to pull a train, the boiler must also supply saturated steam to locomotive appliances for train operation. In the past, **San Juan** passenger trains on the D&RGW were heated by steam from the locomotives. Compressed air is needed to operate the brakes and engine appliances, so steam-powered air pumps are located on the left side of K-36 engines and mounted on the front of the smoke box on the K-28s. These devices, made up of small cylinders and pipes that often leak steam and water, make a characteristic "ka-thunk-ka-thunk" sound.

Each locomotive carries its own electrical system. Just ahead of the engine cab is a steam-powered generator, or dynamo. The generator supplies about 500 Watts at 32 volts DC to operate the headlight, the back up light on the tender, the markers on the engine and tender, and the lamps in the engine cab.

Beneath the couplers on each car and on the engine are large rubber hoses that are connected to form a continuous air line from the engine to the rear of the train. Railroad brakes operate differently from automobile brakes, however. When you step on the brake pedal of your car, you increase the pressure in the brake system. On a train, 70 to 90 pounds per square inch (psi) of air pressure is maintained in the air line while the train is moving. When the engineer operates the brake valve in the locomotive cab, air pressure is reduced in the brake pipe. This causes the brake rigging underneath the car to force the brake shoes against the wheels, thus slowing the train. If the air line is opened or broken anywhere along the train, the brakes will "go into emergency" and the train will stop until the line is again closed and repressurized. The train crew can also "pull the air" from the rear of the train in an emergency. Owing to the hazards of mountain railroading, in 1872 the D&RG became the first U.S. railroad to use air brakes on its freight equipment. The early "straight" air brakes, however, operated by increasing rather than reducing brake pipe pressure. Since the early 1980s the D&SNG has used an additional modified straight-air braking system to enhance operations.

This brief explanation of how the engine works may help you understand how difficult and expensive it is to keep a locomotive operating. Replacement parts can no longer be ordered from Baldwin or other manufacturers, which means those parts must be fabricated in the machine shop. Just be glad that the talented and dedicated roundhouse crew gladly perform the necessary maintenance and servicing tasks.

The locomotive that will pull your train will be one of two classes of engines operated by the D&SNG. They carry the same road numbers and class designations as they did on the Denver and Rio Grande Western. In the North American system, steam engines are classified by the arrangement of their wheels and by the amount of tractive effort.

The D&RGW class designations, such as 'K-36', indicate the engines' wheel arrangement and tractive effort. Tractive effort is the pull in thousands of pounds available at the tender drawbar on clean, dry, and sanded steel rail. The letter 'K' indicates a 2-8-2 wheel arrangement and was adopted by many American railroads to stand for the nickname "Mikado," which originated because the first 2-8-2s built were standard gauge engines purchased by the Japanese Government. The '36' in the class designation means the locomotive has a starting tractive effort of 36,000 pounds. A 2-8-2 engine has two non-powered pilot wheels in front, eight powered drive wheels, and two non-powered trailing wheels.

The original locomotives used on the Silverton Branch were much smaller and pulled with less tractive effort than those used today. Small, lightweight 2-6-0 Moguls and 4-4-0 Americans were the first locomotives used by the D&RG. Later, scores of 4-6-0 Ten-Wheelers and 2-8-0 Consolidations were used throughout the narrow gauge system. On display at Durango's Santa Rita Park is engine No. 315, a 2-8-0 originally built for the Florence and Cripple Creek Railroad that ended its career as the switch engine for the Durango yards. Another example is No. 42, owned by the D&SNG.

By the 1930s, 2-8-2 Mikados of the K-27 class (numbered 450-464 and nicknamed "mudhens") were the primary power for the Silverton Branch, particularly numbers 453 and 463. All of the narrow gauge 2-8-2s were 'outside frame,' which means the driving wheels are inside of the locomotive frame with axles that extend outside to the drive rods. This arrangement, never used for standard gauge engines, allowed the locomotives to be heavier and wider and still negotiate narrow gauge track.

Running gear of engine 476, showing the outside frame, drive rods, valve gear, cranks, and counterweights. Cooling pipes and air tank are just above the frame. The fake diamond-shaped stack, just a metal shroud added for a movie in 1956, had no functionality and was removed by the D&SNG in 1981. (F.W. Osterwald)

*Opening day in Silverton, May 2, 1992. The **First Silverton Train** had backed down to the wye, turned, and was waiting for passengers to load for the return trip to Durango. On the right, the second section of the train is arriving. Note the "bear trap" cinder catcher on the smokestack of number 481.* (Ren Osterwald)

470-Series, Class K-28

Ten engines of the 470-series K-28s were built by the American Locomotive Co. in New York in 1923 for the D&RGW. These engines, which weigh 127 tons and pull with 27,500 lb of effort, were designed for passenger service and were termed "sport models" by the D&RGW crews. Only three of these engines still exist, numbers 473, 476, and 478, and all are owned by the D&SNG. The seven other K-28s were requisitioned by the U.S. Army in 1942 for use on the White Pass & Yukon Railroad in Alaska during World War II, and all were scrapped by 1946.

Engines 473, 476, and 478 saw passenger service on many parts of the Rio Grande's narrow gauge system. The 473 was commonly assigned to the "Chili Line" from Antonito, Colorado, to Santa Fe, New Mexico, as the Santa Fe branch was called, until it was abandoned in 1941. The 476 and 478 regularly pulled the **San Juan**, a daily deluxe passenger train between Alamosa and Durango, until it was discontinued in 1951. When not in passenger service, the K-28s occasionally pulled freight between Durango and Alamosa, normally assigned to the heavier K-36 and K-37 engines.

The 470s are well-known from their long years of service on **The Silverton**, especially from the 1950s until 1980 while they were the sole motive power for the train   and the starring attractions for tourists. Their appearance when new was somewhat different than in more recent years, as shown in the builder's photo of the 470, p. 130, and the picture of 478 in 1951 on p. 131. Movie studios have at times attempted to make the engines look older for old West movies by attaching fake smoke stacks, oil lamps, and wooden pilots, and with gaudy paint (see photo p. 131), but even a casual glance shows that the "sport models" could never pass as a tiny 1880s-era 4-6-0. Still, the D&RGW thought that the shrouds added around the smoke stacks added to the value as a tourist attraction and they became standard equipment for the engines until they were sold to D&SNG.

480-Series Class K-36

The last new narrow gauge locomotives in the U.S. were built by the Baldwin Locomotive Works in Philadelphia, Pennsylvania in 1925 for the D&RGW as the 480-series K-36s (see builder's photo, p. 133). These 10 engines weighed 143 tons with loaded tenders, and pulled with 36,200 lb of tractive effort. Engine numbers 480, 481, 482, and 486 are owned by the D&SNG. Five others, numbers 483, 484, 487, 488, and 489, are owned by the Cumbres & Toltec Scenic Railroad. The 485 was dismantled by the D&RGW in 1955 after it was wrecked in Salida. The 480s had a reputation among railroaders of being the best narrow gauge engines ever owned by the Rio Grande, and one of the most efficient designs of either gauge.

SPECIFICATIONS

Gauge	3'-0"
Valve Gear	Walschaert
Wheels	44" Spoke
Grates	Rosebud
Grate Area — Sq. Ft.	30.1
Superheater	Schmidt Type A
Firebox Size, Inside	72⅛" x 60¼"
Tubes, 2¼" Dia., No.	106
Flues, 5½" Dia., No.	22
Flues, Length over Sheets	16'-0"
Grate Surface, Sq. Ft.	30.17
Width Over Running Boards	9'-5"
Cylinders, Bore	18"
Cylinders, Stroke	22"
Width Over Cylinders	10'-5½"
Width Over Frames	4'-9"
Heating Surface, Firebox	Sq. Ft. 102
Heating Surface, Tubes	Sq. Ft. 994
Heating Surface, Flues	Sq. Ft. 1,600
Superheater Surface	Sq. Ft. 396
Tractive Power	Lbs. 27,500
Wt. on Engine Truck	Lbs. 20,500
Wt. on First Drivers	Lbs. 29,200
Wt. on Second Drivers	Lbs. 29,200
Wt. on Third Drivers—Main	Lbs. 27,600
Wt. on Fourth Drivers	Lbs. 27,500
Wt. on Trailer Axle	Lbs. 22,000
Wt. on Drivers—Total	Lbs. 113,500
Wt. of Engine	Lbs. 156,000
Wt. of Tender—Loaded	Lbs. 98,500
Wt. of Engine & Tender—Loaded	Lbs. 254,500
Wheelbase, Driving	12'-3"
Wheelbase, Engine	28'-10"
Wheelbase, Engine & Tender	53'-6"
Boiler, Inside Dia.	63½"
Boiler Pressure	Psi 200
Factor of Adhesion	4.12

Builders—American Locomotive Co.

Date in Service—October, 1923

Builder's photo and specifications for engine 470, the first K-28 delivered to the D&RGW, in 1923.   (Colorado Historical Society)

Engine 478 beside the Durango roundhouse in September 1951. This is one of the few D&RGW narrow gauge engines to have a power reverse (the short horizontal cylinder immediately ahead of the cab). Compare with the builder's photo of engine 470 on p. 130.

(F.W. Osterwald)

In July 1951, while pulling a freight train loaded with 900 tons of silver ore concentrates bound for Durango, engine 473 encountered a heat expansion kink in the track at mile 483.7 and landed in the Animas River. All the ore cars stayed on the track, and no one was injured. Following the color scheme used by the movie crew of Denver and Rio Grande *(see p. 41), in 1951 the 473 was painted yellow and given a phony diamond stack and oil headlamp in an effort to promote tourism.* *(Collection of Edna Sanborn)*

They work at peak efficiency pulling heavy loads at slower speeds. Several 480s occasionally pulled the **San Juan** passenger train between Alamosa and Durango in the late 1940s and early 1950s.

Engine 480 was returned to service in 1985 after extensive rebuilding by the D&SNG (see p. 140). Number 481 received a major overhaul at the Alamosa Shops in the early 1960s but was never used until it was purchased by the D&SNG.

The 482 pulled the last train northward through the San Luis Valley from Alamosa to Salida in 1952. It was retired by the D&RGW in April, 1959 and stored in Alamosa until 1970, when it was part of the large collection of equipment sold to the states of Colorado and New Mexico for use on the C&TS. In October 1991, the Durango & Silverton traded K-37 engine 497 for the 482 (p. 140).

In 1999, number 486, donated by the D&RGW in 1966 for display at the Royal Gorge suspension bridge near Cañon City, Colorado, was traded for D&SNG's number 499 (which had been operated through the Gorge by the D&RG as a standard gauge 2-8-0). After it was rebuilt in the Durango shops, the 486 made its first run on August 26, 2000 during a RAILFEST event (photos, pp. 138, 139, 163)

K-36 number 486 is sitting on the Durango ready track on a summer day sometime during the 1940s. It is most likely awaiting a trip on the turntable prior to being assigned to an eastbound freight. K-37 number 495 is directly behind the 486. (John W. Hand)

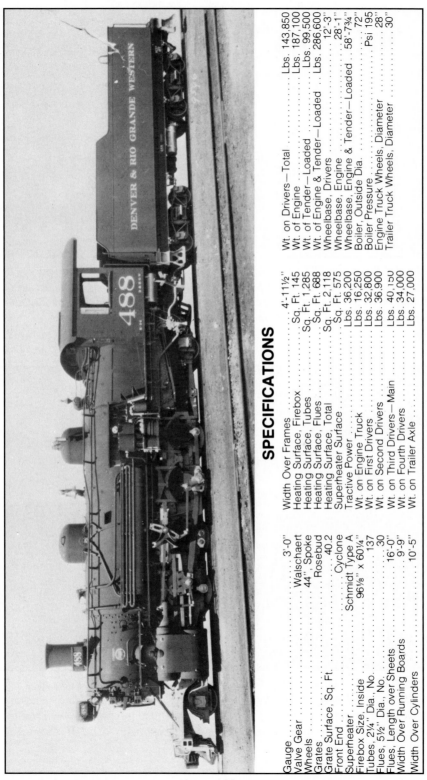

SPECIFICATIONS

Gauge	3'-0"
Valve Gear	Walschaert
Wheels	44", Spoke
Grates	Rosebud
Grate Surface, Sq. Ft.	40.2
Front End	Cyclone
Superheater	Schmidt Type A
Firebox Size, Inside	96⅛" x 60¼"
Tubes, 2¼" Dia., No.	137
Flues, 5½" Dia., No.	30
Flues, Length over Sheets	16'-0"
Width Over Running Boards	9'-9"
Width Over Cylinders	10'-5"
Width Over Frames	4'-11½"
Heating Surface, Firebox	Sq. Ft. 145
Heating Surface, Tubes	Sq. Ft. 1,285
Heating Surface, Flues	Sq. Ft. 688
Heating Surface, Total	Sq. Ft. 2,118
Superheater Surface	Sq. Ft. 575
Tractive Power	Lbs. 36,200
Wt. on Engine Truck	Lbs. 16,250
Wt. on First Drivers	Lbs. 32,800
Wt. on Second Drivers	Lbs. 36,900
Wt. on Third Drivers—Main	Lbs. 40,150
Wt. on Fourth Drivers	Lbs. 34,000
Wt. on Trailer Axle	Lbs. 27,000
Wt. on Drivers—Total	Lbs. 143,850
Wt. of Engine	Lbs. 187,100
Wt. of Tender—Loaded	Lbs. 99,500
Wt. of Engine & Tender—Loaded	Lbs. 286,600
Wheelbase, Drivers	12'-3"
Wheelbase, Engine	28'-1"
Wheelbase, Engine & Tender—Loaded	58'-7¾"
Boiler, Outside Dia.	72"
Boiler Pressure	Psi 195
Engine Truck Wheels, Diameter	28"
Trailer Truck Wheels, Diameter	30"

K-36 engine 488 at the Baldwin Locomotive Works in Philadelphia, built in 1925 for the D&RGW. (Colorado Historical Society)

On May 3, 1981, engine 480 departed Alamosa for the last time. After an overnight stop in South Fork, the low-boy trailer left for Durango at 6:30 a.m. This photo, taken about 7:30 a.m., shows the engine barely had enough clearance to pass through the snowshed near the top of Wolf Creek Pass. The summit was reached about 8:00 a.m. The descent was even slower. (D.B Osterwald)

About 2:00 p.m., the 480 arrived in Durango. This photo was taken just before the truck was backed into a sloping pit dug along the west side of the roundhouse. After matching rails and removing the anchoring chains from the engine, 480 was rolled from the trailer onto the track by releasing the winch cable on the cab of the truck. (F.W. Osterwald)

*After seven years of service on **The Silverton**, locomotive 497 left Durango October 8, 1991, bound for Chama, New Mexico, and service on the C&TS Railroad. This engine has the distinction of being the only K-37 to operate on the Silverton Branch north of Rockwood.*

On October 9, 1991, long-unused engine 482 was loaded on the same low-boy trailer and transported from Chama to Durango. This photo was taken in the Durango yards just before the engine was unloaded. *(Both photos, Amos Cordova)*

490-Series Class K-37

Two 490-series K-37 engines, numbers 493 and 498, are owned by the D&SNG but are currently not used. These engines were built for the D&RG by Baldwin in 1902 as standard gauge 2-8-0s (D&RG Class C-41). In 1928 and 1930, 10 of the C-41s were rebuilt at the Rio Grande's Burnham Shops in Denver into narrow gauge 2-8-2s, with new frames and wheels supplied by Baldwin.

The 490s can be distinguished from the 480s by their old-fashioned fluted (indented) sand and steam domes and by the straight profiles of their boiler tops. These are the heaviest narrow gauge engines and weigh 154 tons with loaded tenders and can pull with 37,100 lb of effort. Look under the tender of a 490-series engine to see evidence of their history—the tender wheels were simply moved closer together to fit narrow gauge track, using the original axles and truck side-frames. Engine 493 is currently on display at the Silverton depot.

A third K-37, number 497, was also sold to the D&SNG in 1981. When the new D&SNG began adding more and longer passenger trains, the railroad had an immediate need for heavier locomotives. The K-36 in the best condition, number 481, was already in use, so in 1984 the 497 was rebuilt and operated for 7 years on the branch. During this time, it was determined that the trailing truck caused problems negotiating the sharp curves in the Animas canyon. As a result, the D&SNG traded the 497 to the C&TS for one of their unused K-36s, number 482 (see p. 135).

Class 70 Engine 42

Engine 42 was one of 6 Class 70 locomotives built in 1887 by Baldwin for the D&RG. This 2-8-0 was originally numbered 420. In November 1916, the engine was sold to the RGS and was used until the railroad was dismantled in 1952. Note that in the subsequent 1924 D&RG renumbering, the remaining Class 70 locomotives became Class C-17. The engine weighs 35 tons and pulls with 17,100 lb of tractive effort.

The last train movement on the RGS consisted of engine 42 with a caboose running from Grady (east of Mancos, Colorado) to Durango.

In 1953, the engine was sold to the Narrow Gauge Motel in Alamosa, formerly owned by Bob Richardson, the founder of the Colorado Railroad Museum in Golden. During 1958, the 42 was sold to the Magic Mountain Amusement Park in Golden, where it was converted to burn fuel oil and operated briefly. In 1969, it found a new home in Monument, Colorado, where it was on display in front of a bank. Engine 42 returned to Golden in 1971 as part of a restaurant display at Heritage Square and remained there until it was purchased by the D&SNG in 1983. It is currently part of the Durango roundhouse museum.

In July 1938 this northbound Rio Grande Southern freight pulled by RGS No. 42 was leaving Durango with a 12-car train and a helper engine on the rear.

(Otto C. Perry, Denver Public Library, West. History Dept.)

By August of 1954 RGS engine 42 was repainted and on display at Robert Richardson s Narrow Gauge Motel in Alamosa, along with a stock car and RGS caboose No. 0404.

(Richard H. Kindig, Courtesy Sundance Publications Ltd.)

On August 15, 1998, ex-Rio Grande Southern engine 42 was pulled out of the Durango roundhouse museum and onto the turntable.   *(D.B. Osterwald)*

486 RETURNS TO THE NARROW GAUGE

No. 486 on display at the Royal Gorge Park.

The 486 loaded on the trailer before leaving for Durango, May 20, 1999.

In August 1999, with its boiler jacket removed, the refit of No. 486 is underway.   *(D.B. Osterwald)*

With its exterior restored, K-37 No. 499 has replaced engine 486 on display high above the waters of the Arkansas River in the Royal Gorge. June, 1999.   *(Ann Swim)*

After pulling train No. 463 on its first passenger run, engine 486 rests at Blair Street in Silverton. August 26, 2000.   *(John Selheim)*

ENGINE RESTORATIONS

ENGINE 481

Number 481 received a major overhaul at the D&RGW Alamosa shop in the early 1960s, but never was used again by the Rio Grande. It was pulled westward to Durango in the last Rio Grande narrow gauge freight train over Cumbres Pass in December 1968, and was stored in Durango until it was sold to the D&SNG. After extensive inspection, overhaul, and repair, 481 returned to service in August 1981 (photo, p. 32).

ENGINE 480

At the time of the sale of the Silverton branch, the 480 was stored outside the Alamosa roundhouse where it had sat since its retirement from service on the D&RGW in 1964. In May 1981, it was hauled to Durango by truck.

When the rebuilding was begun, it was found that many parts had to be replaced. New grates, firebox door, Johnson bar, throttle parts, smoke box interior parts, injectors, boiler check valves, pilot, fountain, and snifter valves were located or fabricated. A bell and whistle were found in a box-car of parts left in Durango by the Rio Grande. Many other parts, such as the lubricators and the running gear, needed extensive repairs. On July 13, 1985, engine 480 pulled its first D&SNG revenue train on the afternoon run of the **Cascade Canyon Train** to the Cascade Canyon wye and back. Two days later, it made its first trip to Silverton, pulling the 7:30 a.m. **San Juan Express**.

ENGINE 482

In 1991, the C&TS Railroad Commission and the D&SNG Railroad agreed to trade the D&SNG's fully-operational engine 497 for C&TS K-36 number 482, which had been stored in Chama, N.M. since 1970. A flatbed truck hauled the two locomotives between Chama and Durango in October.

After its arrival in Durango, a hydrostatic test revealed the boiler of 482 to be in excellent condition. The engine was sandblasted, staybolt caps were inspected and renewed, the running gear was overhauled, and intensive repairs were made to the cab, including new woodwork, windows, and doors. Much more work and time were required to restore the 482 than the 480 because so many small pipes and cab equipment were missing and had to be fabricated in the D&SNG shops. After standing idle 33 years, engine 482 began service on May 2, the annual opening day for 1992, pulling the first morning train to Silverton (photos, pp. 128, 135).

Another locomotive swap occurred in May 1999 when the City of Cañon City agreed to trade K-36 No. 486, on display at the Royal Gorge Park since 1966, for the D&SNG's K-37 No. 499. In terms of the history of the D&RGW railroad, the 499 has the distinction of having been used on the line through the Royal Gorge as standard gauge Class C-41, before it was converted to narrow gauge in 1930. The 480s were never used through the Gorge because the narrow gauge track was removed many years before the K-36s were built. On May 20, 1999, the 486 arrived in Durango on a flatbed trailer. The 499 was then loaded on the same trailer and hauled to the rim of the Gorge, arriving on May 25 (photos, pp. 138, 139).

The 486 was immediately placed in the Durango shops for a complete overhaul. It is estimated that more than 10,000 man-hours and $250,000 were needed to restore this locomotive before it was placed in service and made its first run to Silverton on August 26 during RAILFEST 2000 (photos, pp. 157, 163).

PASSENGER EQUIPMENT

The passenger equipment on the Silverton trains, although they all appear to be similar in external appearance, have had long and varied careers in service on the Rio Grande. The passenger cars were built at many different times by different builders and have undergone numerous and extensive rebuildings and renumberings. In 1923, all the D&RGW narrow gauge passenger equipment was rebuilt with reinforced underframes and 26-inch wheels substituted for 30-inch wheels, which lowered all the cars. Some cars have survived train wrecks and fires, and others were converted to outfit (work) cars and then rebuilt and returned to passenger service by the D&SNG, having been extensively rebuilt in the Durango car shop. The craftsmen duplicate missing parts after careful study of original plans, and use as much original material as possible.

If you ride in a closed coach, it may have been built as early as 1879, or as late as 1986. Interiors of the older cars look much as they did in the 1880s, except that carpeting has been replaced with linoleum and the overstuffed plush seats replaced with more durable seats. Coal stoves have been removed from all the coaches, and those cars used for winter runs to Cascade Canyon Wye are heated with a forced-air, propane heating system along the floors and are fully insulated for winter operations. The open observation cars were rebuilt from standard gauge cars by the D&RGW and by the D&SNG.

The origins of some cars are obscure and difficult to determine. Histories of the various cars described below were assembled from many sources, but much of the information was compiled by Jackson C. Thode from data in the D&RGW files (also see the Equipment Roster, pp. 156-157).

Baggage-Concession Car 64 stored beside the car shop awaiting spring and the return of tourists. *(Richard Millard)*

Car 313 in the Durango yards shortly before it went into service in 1997.

(Richard Millard)

BAGGAGE-CONCESSION CAR 64

This car was built by the D&RG in 1889 as a mail-baggage combination car. In May 1983, the D&SNG purchased the car from the Black Hills Central Railroad in South Dakota and refurbished it for use as a baggage and concession car.

Coaches 284 and 327 at the Durango depot in September 1951 painted Pullman green for duty on the **San Juan**. *Coach 284 is now preserved at the Colorado Railroad Museum in Golden, and No. 327 (see p. 148) has been refurbished by the D&SNG and is named* Durango. *(F.W. Osterwald)*

Carman Damon McCadden finishing the interior of car 566 in June 1982. This car has had an interesting career as outlined on p. 149. *(F.W. Osterwald)*

CONCESSION CAR 126

Car number 126 was built by the D&RG in 1883 as baggage car 27. It was renumbered 126 in 1886; at that time it had a clerestory roof with one baggage door per side and no end doors. Train-line steam heat, air and signal lines were added in 1939 so the car could be used on the **San Juan** and **Shavano**. The D&RGW's Burnham Shops in Denver converted it into a snack-bar car in 1963, and converted the car to a coach in 1979 when steel siding, seats and windows were added. The D&SNG reconverted the coach to a permanent concession car in 1982.

D&RGW baggage car 126 in Durango, September 4, 1951. The car had been painted yellow before its appearance in the movie, "Ticket to Tomahawk," but the letterboard just below the roof is still blank.   *(F.W. Osterwald)*

CONCESSION CAR 212

The oldest car in regular use on **The Silverton** trains (and as far as is known, the second oldest railroad car in Colorado) is D&SNG car 212. It was built by Billmeyer and Small in 1879 as a 45-passenger coach, named *Caliente*, and its original number was 20. It was rebuilt in 1887 into a combination coach-baggage car and was renumbered 215. At that time it had a clerestory roof with bullnose ends. The interior of the passenger compartment was finished in ash and the baggage compartment was painted a light green. The 212 underwent some changes later, however, because by 1904 the clerestory roof had duckbill ends and seats for 28 passengers.

The car was used on the Pagosa Springs Branch of the D&RGW for many years and, during that mixed train service, had a caboose cupola, end ladders, roof walks, as well as high handrails. When the Pagosa Springs Branch was abandoned, the cupola was removed and the handrails and roof walk extended for the full length of the car. The car then was assigned to the Silverton Branch. In an interesting turn of events, D&RGW car 215

Combination car 212 in Durango, September 4, 1951, also painted yellow for the movie, "Ticket to Tomahawk." After the movie was filmed along the branch, the D&RGW decided to adopt this paint scheme for all their passenger equipment (including standard gauge) and named it "Rio Grande Gold."   *(F. W. Osterwald)*

became 212. Combination car 215 had been sold by the Rio Grande to a Mexican railroad in 1942, but when the D&RGW discovered that 215 was larger than another narrow gauge combine, numbered 212, the numbers of the two cars were switched and the smaller car was sent to Mexico.

In 1949, the 212 was painted yellow-orange for the movie "Ticket to Tomahawk," which was filmed mostly along the Silverton Branch. At that time the high handrail on the roof was removed. In early 1951, 212, in the new "Rio Grande Gold" paint scheme, became the entire consist of a short train that ran between Chama and Dulce, New Mexico, for a few months after passenger service between Alamosa and Durango was discontinued. The D&RGW was forced to operate the stub train because the New Mexico Public Utilities Commission did not grant permission to abandon the **San Juan** in that state until May 1951. In 1964, the car was converted at the Burnham Shops to a snack-bar car. Number 212 was converted to a coach and given new steel siding at Burnham in 1979. The coach seats were removed to provide more space for the snack-bar by the D&SNG in 1982, and by 1986, it was a concession car.

COACH-BAGGAGE 213

Combination car 213, named *Home Ranch*, was built in 1983 by the D&SNG. It is especially designed so that passengers in wheelchairs can ride the train. Telluride Iron Works in Durango fabricated the steel frame, using D&RGW plans for other cars built during the 1960s. Sliding doors on each side, equivalent to baggage doors on conventional coach-baggage combines, have hydraulic lifts to handle wheelchairs.

COACH 257

Car 257 was built in 1880 by Jackson and Sharp as coach 43 for the D&RG. When delivered, it had duckbill roof ends, but later were covered to resemble bullnose ends when the car was rebuilt in 1886 and renumbered 267. In May 1891, it was sold to the Rio Grande Southern, which rebuilt the car and renumbered it 257. It was used as a coach until some time in the 1920s, when it was converted into a passenger-baggage combination car with two narrow side doors, leaving only about ⅓ of it for passengers; the windows in the baggage portion were covered. Number 257 was retired when the RGS began to operate its famous "Galloping Geese" gasoline-powered railcars in 1931. For 30 years, the car sat without wheels on a farm near Montrose and more recently in Silverton, until the D&SNG obtained the car in August 1983. After a complete rebuilding, the car again has duckbilled ends and prefabricated Buntin-type reversible seats. Car 257 returned to service in 1986 as a coach, named *Shenandoah*.

COACH 270

This coach was built in 1880 at the Delaware Car Works of Jackson and Sharp, as number 46, and named *Galesteo*. It was renumbered 270 in 1886. In 1924, it became a kitchen-diner outfit car numbered 0270. The car was rebuilt by the D&SNG in 1982, and is insulated for winter use. The interior was restored to its original condition except for the floor and seats. The interior has bird's-eye maple panels between the windows. Portions of the original oak and mahogany moldings were preserved, and new moldings were milled to match. All moldings were carefully reinstalled above the windows. Buntin-type reversible seats were redesigned and fabricated by the D&SNG for this coach, using an original Buntin seat in an old work car as a model. The car is now named *Pinkerton*.

COACH 291

Coach 291 was built by Jackson and Sharp in 1881 as coach 67 (without a name). It was renumbered 291 in 1886 and 0291 in 1924, when it was transferred to nonrevenue work service, and then was completely rebuilt in 1984. Named the *King Mine*, it has seats that duplicate the old fashioned reversible ("walkover") seats used in coaches 100 years ago.

COACH 311

Car 311 was built in 1881 by Jackson and Sharp as D&RG coach 87, with a seating capacity of 44 passengers. It too was renumbered in 1887. The interior was finished in oak, and contained 22 Buntin reversible seats, continuous hat racks, oil lamps, and "one large cooler." It was sold in 1944 to the Montezuma Lumber Co. in McPhee, near Dolores. Later, the car was resold and used as a residence. The D&SNG bought the coach in 1982, and after a complete rebuilding in 1984, it was named *McPhee* and returned to service.

D&RGW outfit car 0270, now D&SNG coach 270 (the Pinkerton), *as it looked in February 1969 after many years as a kitchen-diner outfit car.* (R.W. Osterwald)

End view of coach 270 in the D&SNG car shop. The sagging underframe and end platforms had to be completely rebuilt. (F.W. Osterwald)

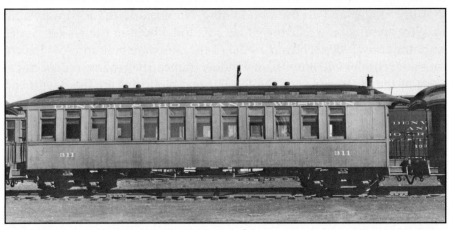

D&RGW coach 311 at Alamosa in 1939. (Turner Van Nort)

COACHES 312, 323, AND 327

These three coaches all were built by the D&RG in 1887 with clerestory roofs and bullnose ends. They were finished in ash and seated 46 passengers. Each was rebuilt in 1937 at the Alamosa shops with vestibule ends, train-line steam heat instead of a coal stove, electric lights, and deluxe Heywood-Wakefield reclining coach seats for 24 passengers. New windows and scribed steel sides were installed at the D&RGW Burnham Shops in 1978-79 to replace the original wooden sides. All were used on the **San Juan** and **Shavano** trains.

Coach 312 replaced another coach which originally had been number 88. The D&SNG named coach 312 the *Silverton*. Coach 323 is named *Animas City*, and Coach 327 is named *Durango* (photo, p. 143).

OPEN OBSERVATION CAR 313

This open observation car was built during the winter of 1987-88 for use with the Animas Canyon Railway diesel bus that hauled hikers and fishermen from Rockwood into the canyon during 1989-91. It was painted red and numbered 1002. The car was stored from 1992-97 until it was rebuilt into open observation car 313. This number was selected because of the car's resemblance to the D&RGW Silver Vista which also bore the number 313 and was destroyed by fire (photo, p. 142).

COACH 319

Coach 319 was built in 1882 by Jackson and Sharp as car number 95. It had a clerestory roof and bullnose ends. By 1886 it was renumbered 319. Through the years it went through the same rebuildings and remodeling that coaches 312, 323, and 327 did. The D&SNG named this car *Needleton*.

COACHES 330-337

Coaches 330, 331, 332, 333, 334, 335, 336 and 337 are slightly different than others coaches owned by the D&SNG. They were built by the D&RGW at the Burnham Shops in Denver and have steel sides made to look like tongue-and-groove wood siding. Numbers 330 and 331 were built in 1963, the first new narrow gauge cars to be built in the United States since the early 1900s. The remainder of the cars were built in 1964. Except for the steel sides and aluminum window frames, they follow the specifications of the older cars very closely. The end platforms are fitted with end posts and ornate guard railings which, as shown in the photos on p. 119, are slightly different from those on older coaches. In 1982, the masonite paneling below the windows was removed by the D&SNG, insulation was installed, and oak paneling substituted. The present name for each coach is on the equipment roster, pp. 156-157.

COACH 460

Coach 460 is the only narrow gauge tourist-sleeper remaining from a group built in 1886 for the D&RG. This coach, assigned to work service in the early 1900s, was used on a D&RGW wrecking train as late as 1957 before it was sold to the Black Hills Central Railroad in South Dakota. The D&SNG purchased the 460 in 1983, but it has not yet been restored.

CONCESSION CAR 566

Car 566 probably was originally mail car 14, built in 1882 by the D&RG, using iron work from Billmeyer and Small. Early D&RG records are difficult to interpret because in 1883, cars were designated as express, baggage, and mail, with each category starting with the number one. In 1886, these designations were changed to express, baggage, postal, and combined mail-baggage-express. Not all the early designations of individual cars carried through to the later designations because of rebuildings, renumberings, scrappings, and destruction by accidents. When former D&RGW outfit car 0566 was being rebuilt by the D&SNG in 1982, the number 14 was discovered on the under frame beams above the trucks. The original configuration was found to be that of a four-door railway post office car when the old siding was removed. According to D&RGW records, the original mail cars numbered 14 to 21 were changed to postal cars and renumbered by 1886. During this renumbering, mail car 14 became postal car number 1—but this didn't last long because it was rebuilt to excursion car 566, probably about 1888. At that time the four side-doors were removed and seats and windows added. As an excursion car it was divided into two compartments, with a table, desk, and two bunks. It was renumbered 0566 in July 1904, and changed from passenger to work service in 1914. By 1920, it was listed as a Bridge and Building Department Foreman coach outfit car. It now serves as a concession car (photo, p. 143).

COACHES 630, 631, 632

Three new coaches, numbers 630-632, the *Hunt*, the *North Star*, and the *Tefft*, were added to the D&SNG roster in 1984 and 1986. The steel underframes and superstructures were built by the Telluride Iron Works in Durango; all other work was done by the D&SNG carmen. These cars all have wood siding.

*Car 404, one of three new open observation cars built in the Burnham Shops in Denver for use on **The Silverton**. This photo was taken May 29, 1967, in Alamosa, shortly after the car arrived on a standard gauge flatcar. It went to Durango on June 12 with the first westbound freight of the year.* (D.B. Osterwald)

OPEN OBSERVATION CARS 400-416

Open observation cars 400, 401, and 402 were originally standard gauge D&RGW boxcars 67191, 66665 and 66271. In 1953, these boxcars were converted into pipe cars numbers 9609, 9611, and 9605, respectively, by cutting down and bracing the sides, removing the ends, and adding narrow gauge trucks. As pipe cars they were used between Alamosa and Farmington, New Mexico during the oil and gas boom in the San Juan Basin in the 1950s. The cars were converted into observation cars by equipping them with passenger car trucks, steel roofs, tile floors, and tramway seats in 1963. Three additional open observation cars, 403, 404, and 405, were built in the Burnham Shops for the 1967 season of **The Silverton**. These were converted from pipe cars 9606, 9600, and 9601, respectively, which were also originally D&RGW standard gauge boxcars in the 66000-66999 series. The trucks for these three cars came from coaches 284, 306, and 320, which were sold to the Colorado Railroad Museum in Golden. Open observation cars 411 and 412 were built between 1982 and 1985 by the D&SNG from pipe cars 9603 and 9608.

Between 1982 and 1986, eleven new open observation cars were built by the D&SNG (Roster, pp. 156-157). Fourteen pairs of passenger trucks were built in 1983 for the new cars and also to replace worn sets on some of the older equipment. Look for the new D&SNG lettering on the truck side-frame castings.

Coach 350 has had an extremely checkered career. The car was built in 1880 by Jackson and Sharp as Horton chair car number 25, carrying the name *Hidalgo*, which reflected the original Rio Grande management's interest in a rail connection with Mexico. It was changed to chair car 403 in 1885. In 1919, it was rebuilt into an office and living car for members of the Valuation Survey who were inventorying the entire railroad property after it was returned to private ownership following World War I. In 1924, the car was converted into a parlor-smoker car. It then became a parlor-buffet car named *Alamosa* (without a number) after a 1937 rebuilding (another car with the same name was destroyed in a derailment on the Rio Grande Southern in 1912). A familiar sight on the end of the **San Juan**, the car had a closed front vestibule, ash interior, steam heat, electric lights, kitchen, buffet, and swivelled, over-stuffed seats for 14 passengers. In 1957, the car was converted to a coach for service on **The Silverton**, and was renumbered 350 and rebuilt with steel siding at Burnham in 1959.

The name *Alamosa* was restored soon after the D&SNG purchased the railroad. During the fall of 1981, the car was reconverted to a parlor car with a bar and small oak tables and chairs for 28 passengers. As an extra fare car, it is used regularly on trains 463 and 464 (**Third Silverton Train**) and on the winter **Cascade Canyon Train**, which runs from Durango to Cascade Canyon wye.

The end platform of coach 350, as it looked in June 1965, with simple railing. This coach, now parlor car Alamosa, *was built in 1880.* (F.W. Osterwald)

Interior of the Alamosa.

(Richard Millard)

The private car Nomad *was restored in the D&SNG car shops in 1998-99 and is now painted tuscan red. This car is available for private charters.*

(©Robert Royem Photography)

PRIVATE CAR *NOMAD*

The *Nomad* (car B-3) was built in 1878 by Billmeyer and Small in York, Pennsylvania, as a Horton Chair Car. It was numbered 16 and named *Fairplay* until 1886 when it was rebuilt by the D&RG and designated business car "N." The car was then part of an Executive Office Train consisting of a kitchen-provision car plus two dining, sleeping and observation cars. This train carried President Taft to the dedication of the Gunnison Diversion Tunnel west of Montrose, in 1909. In 1912, the car was renumbered B-2, a designation that did not last long. (The "B" stood for Business car.) In January, 1917, the B-2, along with B-1 and B-3, were part of a special train of important financiers en route to Durango after inspecting various mining properties near Silverton. Near Bell Spur, at mile 468.4, the entire train, known as the "Millionaire Special," turned over. Car B-2 was at the rear of the train and is reported to have slid 50 ft down the mountain. The other two cars were completely burned, but no one was hurt. The interior of the B-2 was remodelled as an officer's sleeping car at the Burnham Shops and renumbered B-3 in 1917, the number B-2 being assigned at that time to the present *Cinco Animas*. The car was exhibited at the 1949 Chicago Railroad Fair and renamed *General Wm. J. Palmer* for the occasion. It was part of an entire narrow gauge train from the D&RGW, which was lettered for an imaginary Cripple Creek and Tincup Railroad. The B-3 was sold by the D&RGW to a private individual in 1951, resold several more times, and extensively remodeled in 1957. It was repainted a deep green and renamed the *Nomad* sometime between 1958 and 1962. It is the oldest private car now in service in the United States. This car was owned by the Cinco Animas Corporation until 1982, when it was sold to the D&SNG. The interior now has an elegant Victorian decor.

Business Car B-7 was built in 1880 by the Burnham Shops of the D&RG as a flat-roofed baggage car, using ironwork from Billmeyer and Small at York, Pennsylvania. In 1885, it was numbered 116, but the following year it was rebuilt for use as a paycar, designated "R." It is believed that the clerestory roof was added in 1886. In 1946, the B-7 and B-2 (now the *Cinco Animas*) made an official trip over the entire Rio Grande Southern with noted railroad authors Lucius Beebe and Charles Clegg as guests. During yet another rebuilding at the Burnham Shops in 1963, the under frame and trucks were modernized and strengthened, the kitchen was remodelled, and the car was painted yellow and renamed the *General William Jackson Palmer* in honor of the founder of the Denver and Rio Grande Railway. The car is now owned by the D&SNG.

Private car B-7, the General Wm. Jackson Palmer, *has been undergoing restoration in the D&SNG car shops since July 1999. It was found that much of the original exterior and interior wood siding had been ruined by a long-neglected and leaky canvas roof. By March 2001, the new mahogany siding was installed and a new soldered tin roof has replaced the canvas. Most of the original interior fixtures have been restored, including the brass kerosene chandeliers and the nickel- and brass-plated window and door hardware. When completed, the B-7 will also feature modern appliances such as a 20-inch flat panel satellite and DVD television system. It will returned to its original Tuscan red color. (Richard Millard)*

The Cinco Animas *is often chartered for special events. On this occasion the Durango Barbershop Singers entertained before departing Durango.* (Kristi Nelson Cohen)

PRIVATE CAR *CINCO ANIMAS*

This car has a long and involved history. It was built in 1883 by D&RG carmen at the Denver Burnham shops as an emigrant sleeper, number 103. Emigrant sleepers on the narrow gauge had odd configurations internally, with 30 seats below and berths above. Sometime later it was renumbered 452, still as an emigrant sleeper. By 1904, 452 was listed a tourist car. Later it was renumbered 0452 and became an outfit car. It was damaged in a wreck on the Rio Grande Southern Railroad in 1909.

Shortly after this time, a curious switch occurred when a paycar, the "F," was also wrecked. Because of the need to pay railroad employees without delay, the 0452 carbody was refitted internally as a paycar and was placed on the running gear from the "F." As a result of this, the railroad switched the designations of the two cars (the original "F" carbody survived as outfit car 0452 on the Cumbres & Toltec Scenic Railroad).

In 1913, car "F" (ex-0452) became B-5 and was used extensively on both the standard and narrow gauge lines of the D&RG by changing wheel sets in Montrose, Colorado. The car was rebuilt again at the Burnham Shops in 1917 and renumbered B-2 to replace a car destroyed by fire during a derailment near Bell Spur. Vestibules were added to both ends about 1924. The car was sold in 1954 and moved to Oklahoma. In 1963 the car was purchased by the Cinco Animas Corp. at which time it returned again to the Burnham Shops and an open platform with railings replaced the vestibule on one end. The car was also painted tuscan red and received its present name, *Cinco Animas*, for the five individuals who jointly returned it to Durango. In 1982, the corporation sold the car to the D&SNG; it can be chartered as a private car on the end of the Silverton trains.

RailCamp Car 3681

The rolling stock of the D&SNG also includes RailCamp Car 3681, an ex-D&RGW boxcar that was rebuilt by the D&SNG in 1984 and is equipped with a kitchen, a bathroom, and beds. The RailCamp car is pulled to the Cascade Canyon Wye by an extra train on a Monday morning and, for the next four days offers elegant camping. It is available as a charter car for groups up to eight people.

Caboose 0500

This caboose was built by the D&RG in 1886 as caboose number 1. The following year it was renumbered 0500. It worked all over the D&RG narrow gauge system until May 1950, when Robert W. Richardson purchased it for display at his Narrow Gauge Motel in Alamosa. In 1987, the 0500 was sold to a group of Cripple Creek businessmen who had it on display until 1993, when it was acquired and rebuilt by the D&SNG. The interior was restored to the original 1886 appearance. The caboose is also available for group charters.

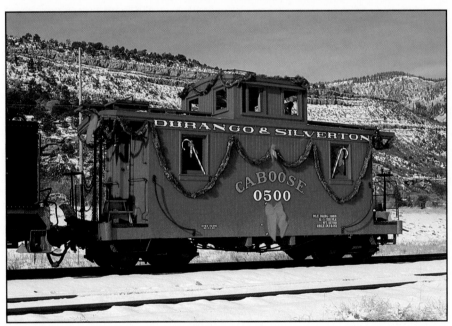

D&SNG short caboose 0500, decorated for a special "Santa Express" train in Durango, December 1993.   *(Richard Millard)*

EQUIPMENT ROSTER

LOCOMOTIVES

IN SERVICE	YEAR BUILT	YEAR REBUILT
473	1923	D&SNG 1989
476	1923	D&SNG 1989
478	1923	D&SNG 1989
480	1925	D&SNG 1985, 1989
481	1925	D&SNG 1981, 1989
482	1925	D&SNG 1992
486	1925	D&SNG 2000

NOT IN SERVICE	YEAR BUILT	YEAR REBUILT
42 (ex-D&RG 420; ex-RGS 42)	1887	
493	1902	D&RGW 1928
498	1902	D&RGW 1930

PASSENGER AND SPECIAL-USE EQUIPMENT

NO.	NAME	PRESENT USE	ORIGINAL USE	YEAR BUILT	YEAR REBUILT	USE AFTER REBUILD
64	—	Baggage-concession	Mail-baggage 64	D&RG 1889	D&SNG 1984	Concession
126	—	Concession	Baggage no. 27	D&RG 1883	D&RGW 1939	Baggage
					D&RGW 1963	Snack-bar car
					D&RGW 1979	Coach
					D&SNG 1982	Concession
212	—	Concession	Coach 20	D&RG 1879	D&RG 1887	Coach-baggage 215
					D&RGW 1942	Coach-baggage 212
					D&RGW 1964	Snack-bar car
					D&RGW 1979	Coach
					D&SNG 1982	Snack-bar car
					D&SNG 1986	Concession
213	Home Ranch	Handicapped access	Passenger-baggage	D&SNG 1983		
257	Shenandoah	Coach	Coach 43	Jackson & Sharp 1880	D&RG 1886	Coach
					RGS 1891	Coach
					RGS 1920s	Passenger-baggage
					D&SNG 1986	Coach
270	Pinkerton	Coach	Coach 46	Jackson & Sharp 1880	D&RGW 1924	Kitchen-diner outfit
					D&SNG 1982	Coach
291	King Mine	Coach	Coach 67	Jackson & Sharp 1881	D&RGW 1924	Non-revenue work svc.
					D&SNG 1984	Coach
311	McPhee	Coach	Coach 87	Jackson & Sharp 1881	D&SNG 1984	Coach
312	Silverton	Coach	Coach 312	D&RG 1887	D&RGW 1937	First-class coach
					D&RGW 1957	Coach
					D&RGW 1979	Coach
319	Needlton	Coach	Coach 95	Jackson & Sharp 1882	D&RGW 1937	First-class coach
					D&RGW 1957	Coach
					D&RGW 1978	Coach
323	Animas City	Coach	Coach 323	D&RG 1887	D&RGW 1937	First-class coach
					D&RGW 1957	Coach
					D&RGW 1978	Coach
327	Durango	Coach	Coach 327	D&RG 1887	D&RGW 1937	First-class coach
					D&RGW 1957	Coach
					D&RGW 1978	Coach
330	Cascade	Coach	Coach	D&RGW 1963		
331	Trimble	Coach	Coach	D&RGW 1963		
332	La Plata	Coach	Coach	D&RGW 1964		
333	Tacoma	Coach	Coach	D&RGW 1964		
334	Hermosa	Coach	Coach	D&RGW 1964		
335	Elk Park	Coach	Coach	D&RGW 1964		
336	Rockwood	Coach	Coach	D&RGW 1964		
337	San Juan	Coach	Coach	D&RGW 1964		
566	—	Concession	Mail 14	D&RG 1882	D&RG ca. 1888	Excursion car
					D&RG 1914	B&B coach-outfit
					D&SNG 1982	Concession
630	Hunt	Coach	Coach	D&SNG 1984		
631	North Star	Coach	Coach	D&SNG 1985		
632	Tefft	Coach	Coach	D&SNG 1986		

OPEN OBSERVATION CARS

NO.	NAME	PRESENT USE	ORIGINAL USE	YEAR BUILT	YEAR REBUILT	USE AFTER REBUILD
313	—	Open observation	Open obs. 1002	D&SNG 1987-88	D&SNG 1997	Same
400	—	Open observation	S.G. boxcar 67191	Pullman 1916	D&RGW 1953	N.G. pipe gondola 9609
					D&RGW 1963	Open observation
401	—	Open observation	S.G. boxcar 66665	Pullman 1916	D&RGW 1953	N.G. pipe gondola 9611
					D&RGW 1963	Open observation
402	—	Open observation	S.G. boxcar 66271	Pullman 1916	D&RGW 1953	N.G. pipe gondola 9605
					D&RGW 1963	Open observation
403	—	Open observation	S.G. boxcar	Pullman 1916	D&RGW 1953	N.G. pipe gondola 9606
					D&RGW 1964	Open observation
404	—	Open observation	S.G. boxcar	Pullman 1916	D&RGW 1953	N.G. pipe gondola 9600
					D&RGW 1964	Open observation

No.	Name	Type	Built as	Builder	Rebuilt	Notes
405	—	Open observation	S.G. boxcar	Pullman 1916	D&RGW 1953	N.G. pipe gondola 9601
					D&RGW 1964	Open observation
406	—	Open observation	S.G. stock car	1937	D&SNG 1985	Open observation
407	—	Open observation	S.G. stock car	1937	D&SNG 1985	Open observation
408	—	Open observation	S.G. stock car	1937	D&SNG 1986	Open observation
409	—	Open observation	S.G. stock car	1937	D&SNG 1986	Open observation
411	—	Open observation	S.G. boxcar	Pullman 1916	D&RGW 1953?	N.G. pipe gondola 9603
					D&SNG 1982	Partial rebuild to 405
					D&SNG 1985	Open observation
412	—	Open observation	S.G. boxcar	Pullman 1916	D&RGW 1953?	N.G. pipe gondola 9608
					D&SNG 1982	Partial rebuild to 406
					D&SNG 1986	Open observation
413	—	Open observation	S.G. stock car	1937	D&SNG 1983	Open observation
414	—	Open observation	S.G. stock car	1937	D&SNG 1984	Open observation
415	—	Open observation	S.G. stock car	1937	D&SNG 1984	Open observation
416	—	Open observation	S.G. stock car	1937	D&SNG 1989	Open observation

SPECIAL CARS

No.	Name	Type	Built as	Builder	Rebuilt	Notes
350	Alamosa	Parlor car	Chaircar 25	Jackson & Sharp 1880	D&RG 1919	Office-living car
					D&RGW 1924	Parlor-smoker car
					D&RGW 1937	Parlor-buffet car
					D&RGW 1957	Coach
					D&RGW 1978	Coach
					D&SNG 1981	Parlor car
B-2	Cinco Animas	Private car	Emigrant sleeper 103	D&RG 1883	D&RG 1909	Paycar "F"
					D&RG 1917	Business car B-2
					Private, 1963	Private car
B-3	Nomad	Private car	Chaircar 16	Billmeyer & Small 1878	D&RG 1886	Business car "N"
					D&RG 1917	Officer's sleeping car
					Private, 1957	Private car
					D&SNG 1987	Private car
					D&SNG 1999	Private car
B-7	Gen. Willam Jackson Palmer	Business car	Baggage	D&RG 1880	D&RG 1886	Paycar "R"
					D&RGW 1963	Business car B-7
					D&SNG 2001	Private car
3681	—	RailCamp car	N.G. boxcar 3681	1903 or 1904	D&RGW 1924	Boxcar
					D&SNG 1984	RailCamp car
0500	—	Caboose	Caboose 1	D&RG 1886	D&SNG 1993	Caboose
0505	—	Caboose		D&RG 1886	D&SNG 1993	Caboose
0540	—	Caboose		D&RG 1881	D&SNG 1999	Caboose

CARS NOT IN SERVICE

No.	Name	Type	Built as	Builder	Rebuilt	Notes
460	—	Coach	Emigrant sleeper	D&RG 1886	D&RG 1903	Construction outfit
					D&RG 1914	Kitchen-diner outfit
					D&RGW 1923	Work train outfit
					BHC 1957	Coach

No. 486 approaching Silverton after an early autumn snowfall in 2000. (Darel Crawford)

The Language of the Rail

By Bob Crabb

One day the switch shanty has a guest.
A young writer who did his best
To grab an earful of the dope,
About the railroad game in hope
Of writing some strong telling tale;
A thrilling romance of the rail.
Notebook in hand and pencil busy,
But all too soon the poor chap's dizzy.

"We're building the local down on two,
So mudhop, start skipping through the dew.
Come on you snakes and show some steam!
Get out that zulu from the team.
Six lion cages, up on number one,
Three merchandise to make the run;
There's two bad orders on the rip,
They are ready now to make the trip."

"OK, ringmaster, let's start the parade!
Get the elephant out of the shade.
Hey tallowpot! Got that teakettle hot?
Come on hoghead get off the spot!
Into the garden take the goat,
A couple of battleships to float.
A flock of straw hats on number three,
And a car of junk for Kankakee."

"A yellow reefer at the dock.
The local's called for nine o'clock,
So toss those buggies into line
And hook the crummy on behind.
The skipper's waiting for the bills,
Highball the baby over the hills;
Just thumb your nose at the rear end shack
As the local freight rolls down the track."

The perplexed writer scratched his head
And then to the fat yardmaster said,
"Kind sir, I find all this confusing,
Won't you explain? Don't be refusing!"
The yardmaster answered with a grin,
"Sure thing, old kid! Don't pull the pin,
Just have a seat and take it slow.
What are the things you want to know?"

"Railroad talk? Our language is queer?
Why! It's all plain English pure and clear.
See those guys at work on the track?
They are gandy dancers with their jacks,
Snipes with king snipe over there,
And that's a car toad bleeding the air
On that long drag down number four.
Well? Do you want to know some more?"

Puzzled, the yardmaster shook his head,
For the writer chap had turned and fled.

(From the Feb. 1930 "Railroad Men's Magazine," re-printed with permission of Carten's Publications)

Glossary

Like so many of the skilled trades in the early days, railroaders developed their own language through the years. Although most are no longer used, you might still hear some of these if you listen closely. This list contains some of the more colorful words and phrases, including most of those used in the poem—enjoy.

AGE: Seniority, or time in railroad service.
AIR MONKEY: Air brake inspector or a carman.
ALLEY: A clear track in a rail yard.
ANCHOR THEM; TIE THEM DOWN: Set the hand brakes.
BAD ORDER: A car needing repair that should not be used.
BATTLESHIP: A superheated locomotive, or a large freight engine.
BEND THE IRON; BEND THE RUST: To change the position of a track switch.
BIG HOLE: The emergency position on a brake valve.
BIG HOOK: The wrecking crane.
BLACK DIAMONDS: Coal.
BLIND SIDING: A siding where both ends are not visible.
BOARD: Any fixed traffic signal.
BOOMER; FLOATER: A railroader who never stayed on one road very long.
BRAINLESS WONDER: An employee who is always making mistakes, or goes about a job the hard way.
BRAINS; CAPTAIN; SKIPPER: The conductor.
BRASS COLLAR; BRASS HAT; BRASS SUITCASE; MAIN PIN: A railroad official.
BRASS POUNDER: The telegraph operator.
BROWNIES: Demerit or bad conduct marks placed in an employees' service record.
BULL; GUM SHOE: Railroad police or the Special Agent.
CRUMMY: The caboose. Also BUGGY; CAGE; CHARIOT; CLOWN WAGON; CRIB; HACK; HEARSE; MONKEY HOUSE; PALACE; PARLOR; WAY CAR.
CAR TOAD; CAR WHACK; CAR TONK: Anyone who repairs railroad cars.
CINDER CRUNCHER: A switchman or a railfan.
CINDER SNAPPER: A passenger who likes to ride on an open platform.
CLUB: A smooth hickory pole used by brakemen to tighten brake wheels.
CLUB WINDER; PIN PULLER: A brakeman.
CORN FIELD MEET: A head-on collision between two trains.
COW CATCHER: The locomotive pilot.
CROAKER: The company doctor.

CUPOLA: A caboose observation tower.

CUSHIONS; VARNISH: Passenger equipment.

CUT: A number of cars coupled together.

DEADHEAD: A firemens' term for a brakeman, or an employee riding back to his home terminal.

DECORATE: Brakemen on the tops of cars.

DETAINER; DELAYER: A train dispatcher.

DIAMOND: A place where two tracks cross each other without any switches.

DOG CATCHER: A crew sent out to relieve another crew whose 16-hour service limit has expired.

DOG HOUSE: On the D&RGW, a heated shelter on the tender from which the head-end brakeman could observe the train.

DRAG: A heavily-loaded freight train.

DRINK: The engine takes water.

DROP: A switching move.

DRUMMER: The yard conductor.

DYNAMITER: A car with a defective brake valve.

ELEPHANT: A road locomotive.

FLIMSY; DOPE: Train orders.

FLOP: A bed in the railroad hotel.

FOG, PUTTY: Steam.

FROG: A tool for re-railing wheels, or the center part of a track switch.

GANDY DANCER; SNIPE: A track worker.

GARDEN: The freight yard.

GATE: A track switch.

GLORY: Accidental death while in duty.

GOAT: A yard engine.

GO HIGH: Climbing on top of a car to pass hand signals.

GUN: A track torpedo, or a locomotive injector.

HEAD MAN: The head-end brakeman.

HERDER; HOSTLER: A railroader that takes care of locomotives at the terminal.

HIGHBALL: A signal to depart immediately.

HIGH IRON; MAIN IRON; MAIN STEM: The main line.

HIGHLINER: A train on the main line, usually a fast passenger train.

HIGH WHEELER: A passenger locomotive.

HIT THE GRIT: Fall off a car.

HOG; JACK; MILL; PIG: A locomotive.

HOGHEAD; EAGLE EYE; PIG MAULER: The engineer.

HOG LAW: The Federal law limiting on-duty time to 16 hours.

HOLE: A side track; a siding.

HOPPER: An open-top car with a drop bottom.

HOT BOX: An overheated wheel bearing.

HOT SHOT: A fast train.

IN THE HOLE: A train waiting on a siding to allow another to pass.

JOHNSON BAR: The engine's reverse lever.

KICK: A switching movement where a car is shoved by the engine and turned loose.

KING: A freight conductor.

KING SNIPE: The track section foreman.

LADDER; LEAD: A main yard track that leads into other yard tracks.

LIGHT ENGINE: An engine moving over the road with no train and no caboose.

LION CAGE; COW CAGE: A stock car.

LOCAL: A slow moving train that does a lot of switching while serving local businesses.

MAKE A HITCH: Couple two cars together.

MANIFEST: A fast freight train usually carrying perishables or critical merchandise.

MUDHEN; SOAK: A locomotive that lacks a superheater.

MUDHOP: A yard clerk.

NO BILL; NO AIR: A non-union employee.

NUT SPLITTER: A roundhouse machinist.

ON THE GROUND: A derailment.

ORDER BOARD: A signal that indicates whether to pick up orders or to proceed.

OUTLAWED: Working longer than the 16-hour Federal time-limit.

PIG PEN: The roundhouse.

PIN: Coupler lift mechanism.

PULL THE PIN: Quit your job.

RATTLER: A freight train.

REAR END SHACK; END MAN: The rear-end brakeman.

RED BALL: A fast freight.

REEFER: A refrigerator car.

RINGMASTER: The yardmaster.

RIP TRACK: A yard track where bad order cars are repaired.

SACRED OX: A helper engine providing extra pull upgrade.

SECTION GANG: A crew of track workers.

SINKER; SMOKER: A private car.

SHUFFLE THE DECK: Switch freight cars.

SNAKE: A yard switchman.

SNOOZER: A Pullman sleeper car.

SPOTTER: A spy employed by officials.

STINKER: A hotbox.

STRAW HATS: Tourists.

STRING: The company telegraph wires.

SWITCH SHANTY: Yard office.

TALLOWPOT: The fireman.

TEAKETTLE: An old or small locomotive.

TORPEDO: A small explosive charge, placed on a rail as a warning, that detonates when the engine runs over it.

TURNOUT: A track switch.

WAY BILL; WILLIE: Conductor's paperwork indicating the contents and routing of freight cars in his train.

WYE: Two tracks in a 'Y' arrangement used for reversing the direction of a train.

ZULU; SIDEDOOR PULLMAN: A boxcar.

SPECIAL EVENTS

The D&SNG offered a number of special events and excursions in 1998 for railfans and visitors that were well-attended. As a result of this success, the following year a group of similar events was organized and given the name RAILFEST. Because the 1999 excursions were even more popular, RAILFEST has become a yearly event, held the third weekend of August.

As a part RAILFEST 1999, ex-Rio Grande Southern Galloping Goose No. 5 is crossing the high bridge below Tacoma during a runby for photographers.

On August 28, 1999, the Eureka was drifting downgrade towards Durango with excursionists in the coach and caboose. This beautifully restored wood-burning 4-4-0 was built for the Eureka & Palisade Railroad in 1875.   *(Both photos, Becky Osterwald)*

Each of the RAILFESTS has included Galloping Goose No. 5 and engine No. 4, the *Eureka*, for series of special excursions that featured runbys for photographers at scenic spots along the railroad.

Goose No. 5 is one seven gasoline-powered railbuses built by the Rio Grande Southern to provide inexpensive passenger, freight, and mail service during the depression of the 1930s. The Galloping Goose Historical Society of Dolores, Colorado owns No. 5 and has restored it to operational condition.

Engine No. 4 is a beautifully restored wood-burning 4-4-0 built in 1875 by Baldwin Locomotive Works for the former Eureka and Palisade Railroad in Nevada. The engine was sold in 1901 to the Sierra Nevada Wood & Lumber Co., and in 1939 it was sent to a scrap yard in San Francisco from which the Warner Bros. film studio rescued the engine.

The *Eureka* appeared in actor John Wayne's last movie, "The Shootist," filmed in 1976, and in 1978 it was sold to Old Vegas, a tourist town in Henderson, Nevada, where it remained until it was burned in a 1985 fire. Las Vegas attorney Dan Markoff then rescued the engine and spent six years restoring the *Eureka* with brass fittings, ornate decorations, gold filigree striping, and a polished walnut cab. In 1994, it was used for producer Ken Burns' documentary film, "The West."

The theme for RAILFEST 2000 was "Return to the Rails" to commemorate the restoration of engine 486. Author and poet James Burke was Master of Ceremonies. He recited his new poem, "Welcome Home Sister 486," so-called because the 486 has been reunited with sister locomotives 480, 481, and 482. Visitors enjoyed the Durango Barbershop Singers along with the dedication and ribbon-cutting ceremonies.

Other events that are normally part of the RAILFESTS include moonlight train rides to Cascade Canyon Station, receptions in the Durango roundhouse museum, book signings, swap meets for railfans, movies, and special charters for various clubs and organizations.

An added bonus for RAILFEST visitors was the chance to photograph the lighted roundhouse just before dark. (Darel Crawford)

A gaggle of Rio Grande Southern Galloping Geese resting in the Durango yards. From left to right, Goose No. 5 is from Dolores, courtesy of the Galloping Goose Historical Society, No. 2 is on loan from the Colorado Railroad Museum in Golden, Colorado, and Goose No. 1 is a faithful reproduction built by Karl Schaeffer of Ridgeway, Colorado, from the few photographs of the original RGS No. 1. (Dennis Boucher)

The D&SNG roundhouse crew make a final check of No. 486 prior to its first run.
(Darel Crawford)

A portion of the large crowd attending RAILFEST *2000 gathered around engine 486 for the dedication and ribbon-cutting ceremonies before departing at 9:30 am for Silverton.*
(Bill Witthans and Jim Ozment)

REFERENCES

GEOLOGY

Atwood, W.W., and Mather, K.F.,1932, Physiography and Quaternary Geology of the San Juan Mountains, Colorado: U.S. Geological Survey Professional Paper 166, 176 p.

Baars, D.L., and Knight, R.L., 1957, Pre-Pennslyvanian Stratigraphy of the San Juan Mountains and Four Corners Area: *in* New Mexico Geological Survey Guidebook, 8th Field Conference, Southwestern San Juan Mountains, Colorado, p. 108-131.

Burbank, W.S., Eckel, E.B., and Varnes, D.J., 1947, The San Juan Region (Colorado): Colorado Mineral Resources Bulletin, p. 396-446.

Cross, Whitman, Howe, Ernest, and Ransome, F.L., 1905, Description of the Silverton Quadrangle, Colorado: U.S. Geological Survey Atlas, Folio 120.

Cross, Whitman, Howe, Ernest, Irving, J.D., and Emmons, W.H., 1905, Description of the Needle Mountains, Quadrangle, Colorado: U.S. Geological Survey Atlas, Folio 131.

Cross, Whitman, and Hole, Allen D., 1910, Description of the Engineer Mountain Quadrangle, Colorado, U.S. Geological Survey Atlas, Folio 171.

Endlich, F.M., 1876, Report (on the San Juan District, Colorado): U.S. Geological Survey of the Territories (Hayden), Annual Report 8, p. 181-240.

Gary, Margaret, McAfee, Robert, Jr., and Wolf, Carol L., editors, 1972, Glossary of Geology: American Geological Institute, Washington, D.C., 805 p.

George, R.D., 1920, Mineral Waters of Colorado: Colorado Geological Survey, Bulletin 11, 474 p.

Henderson, C.W., 1926, Mining in Colorado, a History of Discovery, Development and Production: U.S. Geological Survey Professional Paper 138, 263 p.

Kelley, Vincent, C., 1957, General Geology and Tectonics of the Western San Juan Mountains, Colorado: *in* New Mexico Geological Society Guidebook, 8th Field Conference, Southwestern San Juan Mountains, Colorado, p. 154-162.

_____ , 1957, Vein and Fault Systems of the Western San Juan Mountains Mineral Belt, Colorado: *in* New Mexico Geological Society Guidebook, 8th Field Conference, Southwestern San Juan Mountains, Colorado, p. 173-176.

Kilgore, Lee, W., 1955, Geology of the Durango Area, La Plata County,Colorado: *in* Four Corners Geological Society Guidebook, no. 1, p. 118-124.

Kottlowski, Frank E., 1957, Mesozoic Strata Flanking the Southwestern San Juan Mountains, Colorado and New Mexico: *in* New Mexico Geological Society Guidebook, 8th Field Conference, San Juan Mountains, Colorado, p. 138-153.

Larsen, Esper, S. Jr., and Cross, Whitman, 1956, Geology and Petrology of the San Juan Region, Southwestern Colorado: U.S. Geological Survey, Professional Paper 258, 303 p.

Luedke, Robert G., and Burbank, Wilbur S., 1968, Volcanism and Cauldron Development in the Western San Juan Mountains, Colorado: *in* Quarterly of the Colorado School of Mines, Golden, Colo., v. 63, no. 3, p. 175-208.

Mather, Kirtley, F., 1957, Geomorphology of the San Juan Mountains: *in* New Mexico Geological Society Guidebook, 8th Field Conference, Southwestern San Juan Mountains, Colorado, p. 102-108.

Parker, Sybil P, editor, 1988, McGraw-Hill Encyclopedia of the Geological Sciences, (2d. ed.): McGraw-Hill Book Co., New York, N.Y., 722 p.

Ransome, F.L., 1901, A Report on the Economic Geology of the Silverton Quadrangle, Colorado: U.S. Geological Survey, Bulletin 182, 265 p.

Silver, Caswell, 1957, Silverton to Durango via Railroad: *in* New Mexico Geological Society Guidebook, 8th Field Conference, Southwestern San Juan Mountains, Colorado, p. 75-90.

Stevens, T.A., Schmitt, L.J., Jr., Sheridan, M.J., and Williams, F.E., 1969, Mineral Resources of the San Juan Primitive Area, Colorado: U.S. Geological Survey, Bulletin 1261-F, 187 p.

Stokes, Wm. Lee, and Varnes, David J., 1955, Glossary of Selected Terms: Colorado Scientific Society Proceedings, v. 16, 165 p.

Tewksbury, B.J., 1985, Revised Interpretation of the Ages of Allochthonous Rocks of the Uncompahgre Formation, Needle Mountains, Colorado: Geological Society of America, Bull. v. 96, p. 224-232.

Varnes, David, J. 1963, Geology and Ore Deposits of the South Silverton Mining Area, San Juan County, Colorado: U.S. Geological Survey, Professional Paper 378-A, 47 p.

Wengerd, Sherman A., and Baars, Donald L., 1957, Durango to Silverton Road Log: *in* New Mexico Geological Society Guidebook, 8th Field Conference, Southwestern San Juan Mountains, Colorado, p. 39-51.

Wengerd, Sherman, A., 1957, Permo-Pennslvanian Strata of the San Juan Mountains, Colorado: *in* New Mexico Geological Society Guidebook, 8th Field Conference, Southwestern San Juan Mountains, Colorado, p. 131-138.

Zapp, A.D., 1949, Geology and Coal Resources of the Durango Area, La Plata and Montezuma Counties, Colorado: U.S. Geological Survey Oil and Gas Investigations Preliminary Map 109.

HISTORY

Ayers, Mary C., 1951, Howardsville in the San Juan: The Colorado Magazine, v. XXVIII, no. 4.

Bartlett, Richard A., 1962, Great Surveys of the West: University of Oklahoma Press, Norman, Okla., 410 p.

Bauer, William H., Ozment, James L., and Willard, John H., 1990, Colorado Post Offices, 1859-1989: Colorado Railroad Museum, Golden, Colorado, 280 p.

Bear, Leith Lende, 1985, Trimble Hot Springs, a Historical Tale: Trimble Hot Springs Inc., Durango, Colorado, 40 p.

Bender, Norman J., 1964, History of the Durango Area: *in* Four Corners Geological Society, Durango-Silverton Guidebook, p. 18-29.

Bird, Allan G., 1986, Silverton Gold, The Story of Silverton's Largest Gold Mine: Silverton, Colorado, 152 p.

Darley, George M., 1899, Pioneering in the San Juan: Chicago, Ill.

Hall, Frank, 1895, History of the State of Colorado: v. 4, Chicago, Ill.

Ingersoll, Ernest, 1882, Silvery San Juan: *in* Harpers Magazine, v. LXIV, no. 383, p. 689-704.

_____ , 1888, The Crest of the Continent: R.R. Donnelley, Chicago, Ill., 344 p.

Kaplan, Michael, 1982, Otto Mears, Paradoxical Pathfinder: San Juan Book Co., Silverton, Colo., 284 p.

Logan, Kenneth, J., 1962, The History of La Plata County: *in* The Encyclopedia of Colorado, Colorado Historical Association, p. 278-282.

Marshall, John B., 1962, History of San Juan County: *in* San Juan County. The Encyclopedia of Colorado, Colorado Historical Association, p. 311-316.

Newhall, Beaumont, and Edkins, Diana, E., 1974, William H. Jackson: Morgan and Morgan, Amon Carter Museum, Ft. Worth, Tex., 158 p.

Nossaman, Allen, Many More Mountains, v. I, Silverton's Roots: Sundance Ltd., Denver, Colo., 352 p.

_____ , 1993, Many More Mountains, v. II, Ruts to Silverton: Sundance Ltd., Denver, Colo., 352 p.

_____ , 1993, Silverton's Story: *in* All Aboard, D&SNG Magazine, Starlight Publishing Co., Albuquerque, New Mex., p. 13-16.

Olsen, Mary Ann, 1962, The Silverton Story: Bearber Printing Co., Cortez, Colo., 28 p.

Pinkert, Leta, 1964, True Stories of Early Days in the San Juan Basin: Hustler Press, Inc., Farmington, New Mex., 38 p.

Sarah Platt Decker Chapter, N.S.D.A.R. 1942, 1946, 1952, 1961, Pioneers of the San Juan Country: v. I and II, Out West Printing Co., v. III, Durango Printing Co., v. IV, Big Mountain Press [all volumes bound together].

Silver, Caswell, 1957, History and Folklore of the San Juan Region: *in* New Mexico Geological Society Guidebook, 8th Field Conference, Southwestern San Juan Mountains, Colorado, p. 222-234.

Smith, Duane A., 1980, Rocky Mountain Boom Town, A History of Durango: University of New Mexico Press, Albuquerque, New Mex., 214 p.

_____ , 1992, Rocky Mountain Mining Camps, The Urban Frontier: University Press of Colorado, Niwot, Colo., 304 p.

_____ , Durango Lore: *in* All Aboard, D&SNG Magazine, v. 2, no. 1, Starlight Publishing Co., Albuquerque, New Mex., p. 9-10.

Thompson, Ian, 1964, The Silverton Country. A Historical Sketch: *in* Four Corners Geological Society, Durango-Silverton Guidebook, p. 1-5.

RAILROADS

Anonymous, 1883, Official Railway Guide to Colorado, the East and West: Reprinted 1978 by Mobile Post Office Society, Omaha, Neb. 120 p.

_____ , 1951-1995, Iron Horse News: newsletter of the Colorado Railroad Museum, Golden, Colo.

_____ , 1953, Ghost town and Calico Railway: Ghost Town, Calif., 59 p.

_____ , The Silverton and Rio Grande-Land: in Colorado Annual, 1963, Colorado Railroad Museum, Golden, Colo.,15 p.

_____ , 1964, Along the Narrow Gauge: U.S. Forest Service pamphlet.

_____ , 1966, American Railroad Journal, Golden West Books, San Marino, Calif., 120 p.

_____ , To Silverton in Snow: in Colorado Annual, 1964, Colorado Railroad Museum, Golden, Colo., 15 p.

_____ , Locomotives of the Rio Grande: 1980, Colorado Railroad Museum, Golden, Colo., 96 p.

_____ , 1924, Library of Railway Practice, Modern Locomotive Science, Railway Educational Press.

_____ , 1925, Elesco Locomotive Superheaters, The Superheater Company.

Athearn, Robert G., 1962, Rebel in the Rockies: Yale University Press, New Haven, Conn., 395 p.

Beebe, Lucius, and Clegg, Charles, 1958, Narrow Gauge in the Rockies: Howell-North, Berkeley, Calif., 224 p.

_____ , 1962, Rio Grande, Mainline of the Rockies: Howell-North, Berkeley, Calif., 380 p.

Carter, Kenneth, E., 1964, The Narrow Gauge Lines: in Four Corners Geological Society, Durango-Silverton Guidebook, p. 7-17.

Chappell, Gordon, S., 1971, Logging Along the Denver & Rio Grande: Colorado Railroad Museum, Golden, Colo., 190 p.

Choda, Kelly, 1956, Thirty Pound Rails: The Filter Press, Aurora, Colo., 46 p.

Crum, Josie M., 1956, Rails Among the Peaks, The D&RG in the San Juan Mountains: reprinted from Railway and Locomotive Historical Society, Bulletin no. 76.

Crum, Josie, Moore, 1961, The Rio Grande Southern Railroad: Hamilton Press, Inc., Durango, Colo., 431 p.

Denver & Rio Grande Railroad records and photographs from 1871 to present: Library, Colorado Historical Society, Denver, Colo.

Denver and Rio Grande Western Railroad Company, 1948, Rules and Regulations of the Operating Department.

Dorman, Richard L., 1987, Durango Always a Railroad Town, v. II: R.D. Publications, Inc., Santa Fe, New Mex., 184 p.

Ferrell, Mallory Hope, 1973, Silver San Juan, The Rio Grande Southern Railroad: Pruett Publishing Co., Boulder, Colo., 643 p.

Hauck, Cornelius, W., and Richardson, Robert W., 1963, Steam in the Rockies, a Denver & Rio Grande Roster: Colorado Railroad Museum, Golden, Colo., 32 p.

Hernick, James L. , editor, 1996, Railroad Timekeeping, National Association of Watch and Clock Collectors, 17th annual seminar, Rockford Illinois.

Hungerford, John B., 1955, Narrow Gauge to Silverton: Hungerford Press, Reseda, Calif., 36 p.

Hunt, Louie, 1955, The Silverton Train: Leucadia, Calif.

Johnson, Ralph P., M.E., 1944, The Steam Locomotive, Simmons-Boardman Publishing Company

LeMassena, R.A., 1964, Colorado's Mountain Railroads, v. III: Smoking Stack Press, Golden, Colo.

_____ , 1974, Rio Grande to the Pacific: Sundance Ltd., Denver, Colo., 416 p.

McCoy, Dell and Collman, Russ, 1971, The Rio Grande Pictorial 1871-1971: Sundance Ltd., Denver, Colo., 216 p.

McKinney, Alexis, 1979, The Silverton's Three Private Cars, Legends on Rails: in Colorado Rail Annual no. 14, Colorado Railroad Museum, Golden, Col., p. 9-23.

Meyer, Frederic L., 1902, The Twentieth Century Manual of Railway and Commercial Telegraphy, Rand, McNally & Company.

Ormes, Robert M., 1963, Railroads and the Rockies: Sage Books, Denver, Colo., 406 p.

Osterwald, Doris, B., 1991, High Line to Leadville: Western Guideways, Ltd., Lakewood, Colo., 160 p.

_____ , 1992, Ticket to Toltec (2nd. ed.): Western Guideways, Ltd., Lakewood, Colo.,128 p.

_____ , 1994, Beyond the Third Rail with Monte Ballough and His Camera: Western Guideways, Ltd., Lakewood, Colo., 204 p.

Richardson, Robert W., 1994, Narrow Gauge News: Colorado Railroad Museum, Colorado Rail Annual No. 21, Golden, Colo., 303 p.

Richardson, Robert W., Walker, John S., Jr., and Farewell, R.C., 1991, A Silverton Trilogy: in Coal, Cinders and Parlor Cars: A Century of Colorado Passenger Trains, Colorado Rail Annual No. 19, Railroad Museum, Golden, Colo., 238 p.

Sloan, Robert E., and Skowronski, Carl A., The Rainbow Route, an Illustrated History: Sundance, Ltd., Denver, Colo., 416 p.

Thode, Jackson, C., 1971, A Century of Passenger Trains: in The 1970 Denver Westerners Brand Book, The Westerners, Denver, Colo., p. 83-265.

_____ , 1989, George L. Beam and the Denver & Rio Grande: v. II: Sundance Ltd., Denver, Colo., 280 p.

Wright, Roy V., editor, 1930, The Locomotive Cyclopedia of American Practice, Ninth Edition, Simmons-Boardman Publishing Company

NATURE

Baerg, Harry J., 1955, How to Know the Western Trees: Wm. C. Brown Co., Dubuque, Iowa, 170 p.

Craighead, John J., Craighead, Frank C. Jr., and Davis, Ray J., 1991, A Field Guide to Rocky Mountain Wildflowers: Houghton Mifflin Co., Boston, Mass. 275 p.

Pesman, Walter M., 1988, Meet the Natives (8th ed.): Denver Botanic Gardens, Denver, Colo., 237 p.

Peterson, Roger Tory, 1990, A Field Guide to Western Birds (3rd. ed): Houghton Mifflin Co., Boston, N.Y., 432 p.

Robbins, Chandler S., Robbins, Bertel Bruun, and Zim, Herbert S., 1966, A Guide to Field Identification Birds of North American: Golden Press, New York, N.Y., 340 p.

Wassink, Jan L., 1993, Mammals of the Central Rockies: Mountain Press Publishing Co., Missouli, Mont., 162 p.

Watts, Tom, 1972, Rocky Mountain Tree Finder: Nature Study Guild, Rochester, N.Y., 62 p.

Weber, William A., 1976, Rocky Mountain Flora: Colorado Associated University Press, Boulder, Colo., 479 p.

Whitley, Stephan, 1985, Western Forests: Alfred Knopf, Inc., New York, N.Y., 670 p.

Yocom, Charles, Weber, William, Beidleman, Richard, and Malick, Donald, 1969, Wildlife and Plants of the Southern Rocky Mountains, Naturegraph Company, Hearldsburg, Calif., 132 p.

NEWPAPERS

Alamosa Journal	Durango Herald
Colorado Chieftan, Pueblo	Durango Idea
Colorado Springs Gazette	Durango Record
Denver Post	Durango Southwest
Denver Republican	La Plata Miner, Silverton
Denver Tribune	The Silverton Standard and the Miner
Durango Democrat	Ouray Times
Durango Evening Herald	San Luis Valley Courier, Alamosa
Durango Daily Herald	The Southwest, Animas City

SOURCES FOR GUIDE MAPS

U.S.Geological Survey 72° quadrangle maps

The geology was compiled from the following maps and supplemented with personal field work:

U.S. Geological Survey, Folios, 120, 131, 171; Professional Papers 258, Plate I, 378-A, Plate I:, Oil & Gas Investigations, Preliminary Map 109.

Four Corners Geological Society, Durango-Silverton Guidebook, p. 67-71.

INDEX

Numbers in boldface are photographs